TRADITIONS OF HOME

COOKIES & MUFFINS

BY MARG RUTTAN

Front Cover, clockwise from lower right
Chocolate Chips Supreme, page 52
Apple Cookies, page 32
Orange Raisin Drops, page 39

**Traditions of Home – Cookies & Muffins
By Marg Ruttan**

Second Printing – November 1994

Traditions of Home Publishing
5134 – 13th Avenue
Edson, Alberta
Canada T7E 1H5

Canadian Cataloguing in Publication Data

Ruttan, Marg, 1949 -

Cookies & muffins

(Traditions of home ; 1)
ISBN 1-895292-11-5

1. Cookies. 2. Muffins. 3. Baking. I. Title. II. Series.

TX772.R87 1992   641.8'654   C92-098049-X

Dishes and Accessories Compliments of:
Eaton's
Edson Jewellery & Gifts
Yellowhead Florists
Stedmans, Edson

Cover Design by:
Amanda Maslany Design
Regina, Saskatchewan

Photography by:
Merle Prosofsky Photography Ltd.
Edmonton, Alberta

Designed, Printed and Produced in Canada by:
Centax Books, a Division of PrintWest Communications Ltd.
Publishing Director, Photo Designer & Food Stylist: Margo Embury
1150 Eighth Avenue, Regina, Saskatchewan, Canada S4R 1C9
(306) 525-2304 FAX (306) 757-2439

T A B L E   O F   C O N T E N T S

Recipes have been tested in U.S. Standard measurements. Common metric measurements are given as a convenience for those who are more familiar with metric. Recipes have not been tested in metric.

INTRODUCTION

Marg Ruttan was born and raised in Gaspé, Quebec. Born into a family tradition of professional cooks, including her mother, grandmothers, grandfather and several uncles, cooking and baking have always been natural and essential ingredients in her life. This creative enjoyment of food is a family tradition that she loves and is now fostering in her own children.

Marg has also lived in Montreal; Cambridge, Ontario and now resides in Edson, Alberta. She has continued to experiment with and enjoy cooking, and she has authored a weekly cooking column for several newspapers.

Good family fare, with all its many comforting flavors and fragrances, is the focus of Marg's culinary artistry. Over the years she has adapted, invented and collected recipes which are true flavor feasts. *Traditions of Home — Cookies & Muffins* is the first in a series of books which will delight and satisfy your taste buds. Savoring the aromas and tastes in *Traditions of Home* will soon become your favorite family tradition.

DEDICATION

For my husband, Fred and our children, Winston, Stacy and Charlotte, who all love good food and enjoy cooking. And for Roger, who has adopted our whole family.

SUGAR 'N' SPICE

BEST EVER SHORTBREAD

Simple and easy to make, these shortbread cookies are always a hit. They're great for Christmas, but I make them all year round.

1½ cups	butter	375 mL
¾ cup	icing sugar	175 mL
2½ cups	all-purpose flour	625 mL

Preheat oven to 350°F (180°C). In a large bowl, cream butter and icing sugar together. Gradually mix in flour. Force dough through cookie press on ungreased cookie sheets. Bake on middle rack for 5-6 minutes.
Makes about 5 dozen. These cookies freeze well.

VARIATIONS:

Cherry Shortbread: Place half a cherry on top of each cookie before baking.

Apricot Shortbread: Cool cookies. Ice bottoms of half of the cookies with apricot jam and top them with the remaining cookies.

Chocolate Shortbread: Ice shortbread with chocolate icing and top with half a cherry.

Ginger Shortbread: These won't go through the cookie press but you can make them as drop cookies. The flavor is superb. Add ½-¾ cup (125-175 mL) well-drained chopped candied ginger to dough after flour is mixed in.

CHOCOLATE ICING I

¼ cup	soft butter	60 mL
1 cup	icing sugar	250 mL
2 tbsp.	cocoa	30 mL

In a small bowl, cream butter, icing sugar and cocoa.

NOTE: If you don't have a cookie press, these cookies can be made by rolling the dough into 1" (2.5 cm) balls and, with the tines of a fork which has been dipped in flour, pressing them into small circles.

See photograph on page 17.

A L M O N D   C R E S C E N T S

A GREAT SHORTBREAD-TYPE COOKIE WITH A SUPERB ALMOND FLAVOR. GREAT FOR CHRISTMAS OR ANY OTHER SPECIAL OCCASION.

1 cup	butter	250 mL
¼ cup	icing sugar	60 mL
1 tsp.	almond extract	5 mL
2 cups	all-purpose flour	500 mL
1 cup	ground almonds	250 mL

Preheat oven to 350°F (180°C). In a medium-sized bowl, combine butter and icing sugar. Mix in almond extract. Gradually work in flour. Stir in ground almonds. Form dough into small cylinders, about the size of your little finger. Bend each cylinder around your finger to form a crescent. Bake on ungreased cookie sheets on middle rack for 8-10 minutes.
Makes 4½ dozen. These cookies freeze well.

VARIATIONS:
When baked, dredge Almond Crescents with icing (confectioner's) sugar.

ORANGE KISSES

A SHORTBREAD-TYPE COOKIE WITH SUPERB FLAVOR. THIS IS AN EASY COOKIE TO MAKE AND IS ALWAYS A HIT.

1 cup	butter	250 mL
½ cup	icing sugar	125 mL
1¾ cups	all-purpose flour	425 mL

Preheat oven to 375° (190°C). In a medium-sized bowl, cream butter and icing sugar together. Gradually mix in flour. Form dough into 1" (2.5 cm) balls and place on ungreased cookie sheets. With the tines of a fork which has been dipped in flour, gently press balls into 1½" (4 cm) circles . Bake on middle rack for 5-6 minutes. When cool frost with Orange Cream Frosting. **Makes about 4½ dozen. These cookies can be frozen and then iced when thawed.**

ORANGE CREAM FROSTING

2 tbsp.	soft butter	30 mL
1 cup	icing sugar	250 mL
2 tbsp.	orange juice	30 mL

Cream together butter, icing sugar and orange juice. Frost cooled cookies.

VARIATION:

Lemon Shortbread: Add 2 tbsp. (30 mL) finely grated lemon rind to batter mixture and substitute 2 tbsp. (30 mL) lemon juice for orange juice in the icing recipe.

See photograph on the back cover.

M A R M A L A D E   C O O K I E S

THESE COOKIES HAVE A RICH, TANGY FLAVOR THAT IS DELICIOUS.
THEY'RE A REAL TREAT.

½ cup	butter or margarine	125 mL
¼ cup	packed brown sugar	60 mL
1	egg, separated	1
1 tsp.	vanilla	5 mL
½ tsp.	salt	2 mL
1½ cups	all-purpose flour	375 mL
½ cup	graham cracker crumbs	125 mL
	marmalade	

Preheat oven to 350° (180°C). In a large bowl, cream butter and sugar
together. Add egg yolk and beat thoroughly. Stir in vanilla and salt.
Gradually mix in flour. Form dough into 1" (2.5 cm) balls and dip into
slightly beaten egg white. Roll in graham cracker crumbs and place on
ungreased cookie sheets. Gently press a finger into the centre of each ball to
make a hollow. Fill hollows with marmalade. Bake on middle rack for 12-15
minutes.
Makes 3 dozen.

VARIATIONS:
Substitute cornflakes or crushed nuts for the graham cracker crumbs.

T H I M B L E   C O O K I E S

WE'VE BEEN MAKING THESE COOKIES IN OUR FAMILY FOR YEARS. THEY'RE DELICIOUS FILLED WITH ANY VARIETY OF JAM OR JELLY. WE ESPECIALLY LIKE CRAB APPLE, RASPBERRY, AND GRAPE JELLY OR THICK STRAWBERRY JAM. ADD THESE TO YOUR CHRISTMAS BAKING.

1 cup	butter*	250 mL
1 cup	granulated sugar	250 mL
2	eggs	2
½ tsp.	vanilla	2 mL
1 tsp.	baking soda	5 mL
½ tsp.	cream of tartar	2 mL
½ tsp.	salt	2 mL
2½ cups	all-purpose flour	625 mL
1½ cups	jam or jelly	375 mL

In a large bowl, cream butter and sugar together. Add eggs and beat thoroughly. Stir in vanilla, baking soda, cream of tartar and salt. Gradually mix in flour. Chill dough in refrigerator for 15 minutes. Preheat oven to 375°F (190°C). Form dough into 1" (2.5 cm) balls and place on ungreased cookie sheets. Dip a thimble in flour and then gently press it into the centre of each ball, making a deep indentation, not cutting all the way through the ball. Fill indentations with your favorite jam or jelly. Bake on middle rack for 7-9 minutes.

Makes 7-8 dozen. These cookies freeze well.

* These cookies can be made with margarine instead of butter but the flavor isn't quite as good.

R A S P B E R R Y   R O U N D S

A VERY ATTRACTIVE COOKIE WITH GREAT FLAVOR. WHILE IT DOES REQUIRE A BIT OF FUSSING, IT'S WELL WORTH THE EFFORT.

1 cup	butter	250 mL
1¼ cups	granulated sugar	300 mL
2	eggs	2
½ tsp.	vanilla	2 mL
1 tsp.	baking soda	5 mL
½ tsp.	cream of tartar	2 mL
½ tsp.	salt	2 mL
2¾ cups	all-purpose flour	675 mL
½ cup	shredded coconut	125 mL
	raspberry jam	
	coconut	

Preheat oven to 375°F (190°C). In a large bowl, cream butter and sugar together. Add eggs and beat thoroughly. Stir in vanilla, baking soda, cream of tartar and salt. Gradually mix in flour. Stir in coconut. Roll dough on a floured surface to ⅛" (3 mm) thickness. Cut 3" (7 cm) rounds from dough. Set aside ½ of the rounds. With the remaining rounds, using a thimble, cut out a 1" (2.5 cm) circle from the centre of each round. Place on ungreased cookie sheets. Bake on middle rack for 5-6 minutes. Cool cookies. Spread the solid rounds with raspberry jam. Place the cut out rounds on top of the jam-covered rounds. Top with Marshmallow Topping, then sprinkle with coconut.
Makes 3½ dozen large cookies.

MARSHMALLOW TOPPING

2 cups	marshmallows	500 mL
2 tbsp.	soft butter	30 mL
1 tbsp.	milk	15 mL
1 tbsp.	honey	15 mL
3	drops red food coloring	3

In saucepan over low heat, melt marshmallows, butter, milk and honey . Add food coloring. Spread over cooled cookies.

C I N N A M O N   D E L I G H T S

THIS IS PROBABLY MY FAVORITE COOKIE. THE CINNAMON FLAVOR IS TRULY DELICIOUS AND THE COOKIE IS DELICATE AND CRUNCHY.

1 cup	butter*	250 mL
1½ cups	granulated sugar	375 mL
2	eggs	2
½ tsp.	vanilla	2 mL
1 tsp.	baking soda	5 mL
½ tsp.	cream of tartar	2 mL
½ tsp.	salt	2 mL
2¾ cups	all-purpose flour	675 mL
3 tbsp.	granulated sugar	45 mL
2 tsp.	cinnamon	10 mL

Preheat oven to 350°F (180°C). In a large bowl, cream butter and sugar together. Add eggs and beat thoroughly. Stir in vanilla, baking soda, cream of tartar and salt. Gradually mix in flour. In a separate bowl, mix sugar and cinnamon together. Set aside. Form dough into 1" (2.5 cm) balls and place on ungreased cookie sheets. Using the tines of a fork which has been dipped in flour, gently press balls into 1½" (4 cm) circles. Sprinkle each circle with sugar and cinnamon mixture. (I use a spare salt or sugar shaker for this purpose.) Bake on middle rack for 8-10 minutes.
Makes 6 dozen. These cookies freeze well.

* These cookies can be made with margarine instead of butter but the flavor isn't quite as good.

See photograph on page 17.

M E L T I N G M O M E N T S

My sister started making these cookies years ago and I enjoyed them so much that I got her recipe. I've been making them ever since and we always have a good supply around, especially at Christmas time. These cookies really do have "melt-in-your-mouth goodness".

1 cup	butter or margarine	250 mL
¾ cup	packed brown sugar	175 mL
1	egg	1
1 tsp.	vanilla	5 mL
½ tsp.	baking soda	2 mL
½ tsp.	baking powder	2 mL
¼ tsp.	salt	1 mL
2 cups	all-purpose flour	500 mL
	cherry halves, pecan halves,	
	slivered almonds and cake decorations	

Preheat oven to 350°F (180°C). In a large bowl, cream butter and sugar together. Add egg and beat thoroughly. Stir in vanilla, baking soda, baking powder and salt. Gradually mix in flour. Form dough into 1" (2.5 cm) balls and place on ungreased cookie sheets. Using the tines of a fork which has been dipped in flour, gently press balls into small circles. Decorate each circle with cherry halves, pecan halves, almond slivers or sparkly cake decorations. Bake on middle rack for 7-8 minutes.

Makes 5 dozen. These cookies freeze well.

BUTTER 'N' SUGAR CRISPS

IN MY FAMILY, WE HAVE BEEN MAKING THESE COOKIES FOR YEARS. THEY'RE TRULY A LOVELY SUGAR COOKIE, CRISP AND DELICATE. MARGARINE CAN BE SUBSTITUTED FOR BUTTER IN THIS RECIPE BUT THE RICH FLAVOR OF BUTTER IS PREFERRED.

1 cup	butter	250 mL
1 cup	granulated sugar	250 mL
2	eggs	2
½ tsp.	vanilla	2 mL
1 tsp.	baking soda	5 mL
½ tsp.	cream of tartar	2 mL
½ tsp.	salt	2 mL
2½ cups	all-purpose flour	625 mL

Preheat oven to 375°F (190°C). In a large bowl, cream butter and sugar together. Add eggs and beat thoroughly. Stir in vanilla, baking soda, cream of tartar and salt. Gradually mix in flour. Form dough into 1" (2.5 cm) balls and place on ungreased cookie sheets. Using the tines of a fork which has been dipped in flour, gently press each ball into a 1½" (4 cm) circle. Bake on middle rack for 5-6 minutes.

Makes about 5 dozen. These cookies freeze well.

VARIATIONS:

Top each cookie with half a cherry, shredded coconut or slivered nuts.

Shape cookies into fingers and, when cooled, dip 1 end of each cookie into melted, semisweet chocolate.

This dough is ideal for use in a cookie press.

See photograph on page 35.

BROWN SUGAR COOKIES

A REAL OLD STAND-BY RECIPE. MY MOM OFTEN MADE THESE FOR ONE OF HER GRANDCHILDREN. HE WAS ALWAYS ASKING FOR COOKIES WITH "NUSSING" (NOTHING) IN THEM AND THIS WAS A FREQUENTLY USED RECIPE TO FILL THAT REQUEST. I TOO HAVE MADE MOUNDS AND MOUNDS OF THESE COOKIES.

½ cup	butter or margarine	125 mL
1 cup	packed brown sugar	250 mL
1	egg	1
1 tsp.	vanilla	5 mL
2 tbsp.	milk	30 mL
1 tsp.	baking soda	5 mL
2 tsp.	cream of tartar	10 mL
1 tsp.	salt	5 mL
2 cups	all-purpose flour	500 mL

Preheat oven to 400°F (200°C). In a large bowl, cream butter and sugar together. Add egg and beat thoroughly. Stir in vanilla and milk. Mix in baking soda, cream of tartar and salt. Gradually stir in flour. Form dough into 1" (2.5 cm) balls and place on ungreased cookie sheets. Using the tines of a fork which has been dipped in flour, gently press balls into 1½" (4 cm) circles. Bake on middle rack for 6-8 minutes.
Makes 4 dozen. These cookies freeze well.

VARIATIONS:

Add 1 cup (250 mL) of rolled oats or crushed cornflakes when adding the flour.

To decorate these cookies, sprinkle tops with slivered nuts or coconut or place half a cherry and some slivered almonds in the middle of each cookie.

H E R M I T S

HERMITS ARE AN OLD-TIME COOKIE, A FAVORITE OF MANY GENERATIONS. SPICY AND DELICIOUS, THEY ARE A REAL TASTE TREAT. EVERYONE SEEMS TO HAVE A SLIGHTLY DIFFERENT RECIPE FOR HERMIT COOKIES, BUT THE ONE THAT FOLLOWS IS THE FAVORITE AT OUR HOUSE.

1 cup	butter or margarine	250 mL
1 cup	packed brown sugar	250 mL
2	eggs	2
1 tsp.	vanilla	5 mL
1 tsp.	baking soda	5 mL
1 tsp.	salt	5 mL
1 tsp.	cinnamon	5 mL
½ tsp.	nutmeg	2 mL
½ tsp.	allspice	2 mL
2½ cups	all-purpose flour	625 mL
1 cup	raisins	250 mL
1 cup	chopped pecans	250 mL

Preheat oven to 350°F (180°C). In a large bowl, cream butter and brown sugar together. Add eggs and beat thoroughly. Stir in vanilla, baking soda, salt and spices. Gradually mix in flour. Stir in raisins and pecans. Drop by teaspoonfuls (5 mL) on ungreased cookie sheets. Bake on middle rack for 12-15 minutes.

Makes about 3½ dozen. These cookies freeze well.

A Romantic Picnic, clockwise from lower right

Best Ever Shortbread with Chocolate Icing, page 6
Orange Pecan Crisps, page 37
Peanutty Chocolate Balls, page 56
Poppy Seed Cookies, page 27
Cinnamon Delights, page 12
Peanut Butter and Jam Cookies, page 21

C A R A M E L   P E C A N S

A CRUNCHY COOKIE WITH THE MARVELLOUS FLAVOR COMBINATION OF CARAMEL AND PECANS.

½ cup	butter or margarine	125 mL
¾ cup	packed brown sugar	175 mL
2 tbsp.	corn syrup	30 mL
1	egg	1
1 tsp.	vanilla	5 mL
½ tsp.	baking soda	2 mL
½ tsp.	salt	2 mL
1¾ cups	all-purpose flour	425 mL
¾ cup	chopped pecans	175 mL
	pecan halves for garnish	

Preheat oven to 350°F (180°C). In a large bowl, cream butter and sugar together. Stir in corn syrup. Add egg and beat thoroughly. Stir in vanilla, baking soda and salt. Gradually mix in flour. Stir in pecans. Form dough into 1" (2.5 cm) balls and place on ungreased cookie sheets. Flatten balls with the tines of a fork which has been dipped in flour. Bake on middle rack for 7-8 minutes. When cool, frost with Caramel Frosting and top with half a pecan. **Makes 4½ dozen.**

CARAMEL FROSTING I

¼ cup	soft butter	60 mL
1 cup	brown sugar	250 mL
5 tbsp.	whipping cream	75 mL
2 cups	icing sugar	500 mL
½ tsp.	vanilla	2 mL

In a small saucepan, combine butter and sugar. Cook over low heat, stirring constantly, until mixture boils. Remove from heat and let stand for 5 minutes. Stir in cream. Gradually mix in icing sugar. Stir in vanilla. Frost cooled cookies.

See photograph on back cover.

B U T T E R S C O T C H   D R O P S

ANOTHER ALL-TIME FAVORITE COOKIE. AN EASY-TO-MAKE DROP COOKIE TOPPED WITH A SUPER ICING. KIDS LOVE THEM AND SO DO I!

¼ cup	shortening	60 mL
½ cup	packed brown sugar	125 mL
½ cup	soft honey	125 mL
1	egg	1
1 tsp.	vanilla	5 mL
½ tsp.	baking soda	2 mL
½ tsp.	salt	2 mL
½ cup	sour milk*	125 mL
2 ¼ cups	all-purpose flour	550 mL

Preheat oven to 350°F (180°C). In a large bowl, cream shortening and sugar together. Stir in honey. Add egg and beat thoroughly. Stir in vanilla, baking soda and salt. Alternately mix in sour milk and flour. Drop by teaspoonfuls (5 mL) on ungreased cookie sheets. Bake on middle rack for 10-12 minutes. When cookies are cool frost with Caramel Frosting, page 19.
 Makes about 2½ dozen.

* To make sour milk, place 1 tbsp. (15 mL) of lemon juice in a cup (250 mL) and fill with whole milk. Halve amount for this recipe. Buttermilk may also be substituted.

PEANUT BUTTER COOKIES

PEANUT BUTTER COOKIES ARE ANOTHER OF THOSE ALL-TIME FAVORITES. I'VE NEVER TASTED A RECIPE FOR PEANUT BUTTER COOKIES THAT'S QUITE AS GOOD AS THIS ONE. ENJOY!

1 cup	butter or margarine	250 mL
1 cup	packed brown sugar	250 mL
1 cup	granulated sugar	250 mL
2	eggs	2
1 cup	peanut butter	250 mL
2 tsp.	baking soda	10 mL
½ tsp.	salt	2 mL
3 cups	all-purpose flour	750 mL

Preheat oven to 350°F (180°C). In a large bowl, cream butter and sugars together. Add eggs and beat thoroughly. Stir in peanut butter, baking soda and salt. Gradually mix in flour. Form dough into 1" (2.5 cm) balls and place on ungreased cookie sheets. With the tines of a fork which has been dipped in flour, gently press balls into 2" (5 cm) circles. Bake on middle rack for 8-10 minutes, until pale gold in color.

Makes about 7 dozen. These cookies freeze well.

See photograph on page 69.

VARIATIONS:

Peanut Butter and Jam Cookies: Form dough into 1" (2.5 cm) balls and place on ungreased cookie sheets. Dip a thimble in flour and then gently press a deep indentation in the center of each ball with the thimble. (Don't go all the way through the ball.) Fill each indentation with your favorite jam or jelly. Bake on middle rack for 8-10 minutes.

See photograph on page 17.

Peanut Butter Chocolate Chip Cookies: Add 1½ cups (375 mL) of chocolate chips after the flour has been added.

S P I C Y   P U M P K I N   D R O P S

FULL-BODIED FLAVOR ABOUNDS IN THIS DELICIOUS COOKIE. EASY TO MAKE AND MARVELLOUS TO EAT, THESE COOKIES NEVER LAST LONG.

¾ cup	butter or margarine	175 mL
1 cup	packed brown sugar	250 mL
2	eggs	2
1 tsp.	vanilla	5 mL
1 cup	cooked, mashed or canned pumpkin	250 mL
½ tsp.	baking soda	2 mL
½ tsp.	baking powder	2 mL
½ tsp.	salt	2 mL
½ tsp.	cinnamon	2 mL
½ tsp.	nutmeg	2 mL
½ tsp.	ginger	2 mL
2¼ cups	all-purpose flour	550 mL
1½ cups	raisins	375 mL

Preheat oven to 375°F (190°C). In a large bowl, cream butter and sugar together. Add eggs and beat thoroughly. Stir in vanilla, pumpkin, baking soda, baking powder, salt and spices. Gradually mix in flour. Stir in raisins. Drop by teaspoonfuls (5 mL) on ungreased cookie sheets. Bake on middle rack for 10-12 minutes.

Makes 3½ dozen.

HONEY CARROT COOKIES

I CAN'T KEEP THESE COOKIES AROUND MY HOUSE AT ALL. MY YOUNGEST DAUGHTER THINKS THEY'RE THE BEST. A SOFT, CAKE-LIKE COOKIE WITH MARVELLOUS FLAVOR, TOP WITH CREAM CHEESE FROSTING FOR A REAL TREAT.

¾ cup	butter or margarine	175 mL
¼ cup	packed brown sugar	60 mL
½ cup	soft honey	125 mL
2	eggs	2
½ tsp.	vanilla	2 mL
1 tsp.	baking powder	5 mL
½ tsp.	baking soda	2 mL
½ tsp.	salt	2 mL
1 tsp.	cinnamon	5 mL
1 cup	grated carrot	250 mL
1¾ cups	all-purpose flour	425 mL

Grease cookie sheets. Preheat oven to 350°F (180°C). In a large bowl, cream butter and brown sugar together. Stir in honey. Add eggs and beat thoroughly. Stir in vanilla, baking powder, baking soda, salt and cinnamon. Stir in grated carrot. Gradually mix in flour. Drop by teaspoonfuls (5 mL) on greased cookie sheets. Allow at least 2" (5 cm) between each cookie as these cookies tend to spread quite a bit. Bake on middle rack for 10-12 minutes. Frost with Cream Cheese Frosting when cool.
Makes about 2½ dozen.

CREAM CHEESE FROSTING

4 oz.	cream cheese, room temperature	125 g
¼ cup	soft butter	60 mL
½ tsp.	vanilla	2 mL
2¼ cups	icing sugar	550 mL

In a small bowl, cream the cream cheese and butter together. Stir in vanilla. Add icing sugar and mix until thoroughly blended. Spread over cooled cookies.

See photograph on the back cover.

G I N G E R   J A M   J A M S

ONE OF OUR FAVORITE COOKIES AT CHRISTMAS TIME. ANOTHER OF THOSE WONDERFUL RECIPES WITH NO EGG BUT GREAT FLAVOR. USE THIS RECIPE TO MAKE GINGERBREAD MEN.

1 cup	shortening	250 mL
1 cup	packed brown sugar	250 mL
1 cup	molasses	250 mL
1 tsp.	baking soda	5 mL
½ cup	hot water	125 mL
1 tsp.	salt	5 mL
1 tbsp.	vanilla	15 mL
1½ tsp.	ginger	7 mL
5 cups	all-purpose flour	1.25 L

Preheat oven to 375°F (190°C). In a large bowl, cream shortening and sugar together. Stir in molasses. Combine the baking soda and hot water, then add to sugar mixture. Stir in salt, vanilla and ginger. Gradually mix in flour. On a floured surface, roll out to ⅛" (3 mm) thickness. Cut into various shapes with cookie cutters. Place on ungreased cookie sheets. Bake on middle rack for 5-6 minutes. Cool on wire racks and ice with Creamy Vanilla Frosting. **Makes about 7 dozen large-sized cookies. These freeze well.**

CREAMY VANILLA FROSTING

2 cups	icing sugar	500 mL
¼ cup	soft butter	60 mL
1 tsp.	vanilla	5 mL
2 tsp.	milk	10 mL

Combine all ingredients until smooth and creamy. Frost cooled cookies.

S O F T   G I N G E R   C O O K I E S

MY DAUGHTER THINKS THESE ARE ONE OF THE BEST COOKIES EVER AND I MUST SAY THAT I HAVE TO AGREE WITH HER. SOFT AND SPICY, THEY'RE TRULY DELICIOUS.

½ cup	butter or margarine	125 mL
1 cup	granulated sugar	250 mL
2	eggs	2
1 cup	molasses	250 mL
1 tsp.	baking soda	5 mL
1 tsp.	salt	5 mL
1 tbsp.	ginger	15 mL
¾ cup	hot water	175 mL
4 cups	all-purpose flour	1 L

Preheat oven to 350°F (180°C). In a large bowl, cream butter and sugar together. Add eggs and beat thoroughly. Mix in molasses, baking soda, salt and ginger. Stir in hot water. Gradually mix in flour. Drop by teaspoonfuls (5 mL) on ungreased cookie sheets. Bake on middle rack for 10-12 minutes. When cookies are cool, ice with Vanilla Frosting.
Makes 4½ dozen.

VANILLA FROSTING I

1½ cups	icing sugar	375 mL
1 tsp.	vanilla	5 mL
¼ cup	soft butter	60 mL
1 tbsp.	milk	15 mL

Combine all ingredients until smooth and creamy. Ice cooled cookies.

OLD-FASHIONED MOLASSES DROPS

MY SISTER-IN-LAW USED TO MAKE THESE COOKIES WHEN I WAS A YOUNG CHILD AND THEY WERE ONE OF MY FAVORITES. I STILL ENJOY THESE RICH, DARK, FLAVORFUL COOKIES AND I'M SURE YOU WILL TOO.

1 cup	shortening	250 mL
½ cup	granulated sugar	125 mL
1	egg	1
1 cup	molasses	250 mL
1 tsp.	baking soda	5 mL
1 tsp.	salt	5 mL
1 tsp.	cinnamon	5 mL
½ tsp.	cloves	2 mL
¾ cup	hot water	175 mL
3 cups	all-purpose flour	750 mL

Preheat oven to 375°F (190°C). In a large bowl, cream shortening and sugar together. Add egg and beat thoroughly. Stir in molasses, baking soda, salt, cinnamon and cloves. Alternately mix in water and flour. Drop by teaspoonfuls (5 mL) on ungreased cookie sheets. Bake on middle rack for 11-13 minutes.
Makes about 5 dozen.

VARIATION:

Mom's Raisin Cookies: Fold 1 cup (250 mL) of raisins into batter after flour has been added.

P O P P Y   S E E D   C O O K I E S

A SOFT CAKE-LIKE COOKIE WHICH IS ENHANCED BY A BUTTER FROSTING.

¼ cup	poppy seeds	60 mL
½ cup	milk	125 mL
¾ cup	butter or margarine	175 mL
¾ cup	granulated sugar	175 mL
2	eggs	2
2 tsp.	lemon juice	10 mL
2 tbsp.	grated lemon rind	30 mL
2 tsp.	baking powder	30 mL
½ tsp.	salt	2 mL
1¾ cups	all-purpose flour	425 mL
	poppy seeds	

In a cup, pour milk over poppy seeds. Let stand for 30 minutes. Preheat oven to 350°F (180°C). In a large bowl, cream butter and sugar together. Add eggs and beat thoroughly. Stir in lemon juice, lemon rind, baking powder and salt. Stir in milk and poppy seed mixture. Gradually mix in flour. Drop by teaspoonfuls (5 mL) on ungreased cookie sheets. Bake on middle rack for 10-12 minutes. Frost with Butter Frosting when cool.
Makes 3 dozen.

BUTTER FROSTING

½ cup	soft butter	125 mL
1½ cups	icing sugar	375 mL
1 tsp.	vanilla	5 mL
1 tsp.	milk	5 mL
3	drops red food coloring (optional)	3

In a small bowl, cream butter; gradually add icing sugar. Stir in vanilla then mix in milk and food coloring. Spread frosting over cooled cookies. Sprinkle with additional poppy seeds if desired.

See photograph on page 17.

C A R A W A Y   C O O K I E S

FOR THOSE WHO, LIKE MY DAD, ENJOY THE FLAVOR OF CARAWAY, THESE COOKIES WILL BE A DELIGHT. THE CARAWAY GIVES THEM A DISTINCTIVE FLAVOR WHICH IS TRULY DELIGHTFUL AND THE MIXED FRUIT PEEL ADDS RICHNESS AND COLOR TO THIS RECIPE.

1 cup	butter	250 mL
½ cup	granulated sugar	125 mL
½ cup	packed brown sugar	125 mL
2	eggs	2
½ tsp.	vanilla	2 mL
1 tsp.	baking soda	5 mL
½ tsp.	cream of tartar	2 mL
½ tsp.	salt	2 mL
2 tbsp.	caraway seed	30 mL
1½ cups	all-purpose flour	375 mL
1 cup	mixed fruit peel	250 mL

Preheat oven to 375°F (190°C). In a large bowl, cream butter and sugars together. Add eggs and beat thoroughly. Stir in vanilla, baking soda, cream of tartar, salt and caraway seed. Gradually mix in flour. Stir in fruit peel. Drop by teaspoonfuls (5 mL) on ungreased cookie sheets. Allow at least 2" (5 cm) between cookies as they spread quite a bit. Bake on middle rack for 8-10 minutes.

Makes 4 dozen. These cookies freeze well.

FRUIT · COOKIES

B A N A N A   D R O P S

A SOFT CAKE-LIKE COOKIE THAT TASTES GREAT.

¾ cup	butter or margarine	175 mL
½ cup	granulated sugar	125 mL
¼ cup	packed brown sugar	60 mL
2	eggs	2
1 tsp.	vanilla	5 mL
2 tsp.	baking powder	10 mL
½ tsp.	baking soda	2 mL
½ tsp.	salt	2 mL
1 tsp.	cinnamon	5 mL
1 cup	mashed, ripe banana	250 mL
2¼ cups	all-purpose flour	550 mL

Preheat oven to 350°F (180°C). In a large bowl, cream butter and sugars together. Add eggs and beat thoroughly. Stir in vanilla, baking powder, baking soda, salt and cinnamon. Stir in mashed banana. Gradually mix in flour. Drop by teaspoonfuls (5 mL) on ungreased cookie sheets. Bake on middle rack for 12-15 minutes.
Makes 3-3½ dozen.

F R U I T   C O C K T A I L   C O O K I E S

A SOFT, MOIST COOKIE WITH GREAT FLAVOR, BEST WHEN FRESH.

¾ cup	butter or margarine	175 mL
1½ cups	packed brown sugar	375 mL
2	eggs	2
1 tsp.	vanilla	5 mL
1 tsp.	baking soda	5 mL
½ tsp.	salt	2 mL
½ tsp.	cinnamon	2 mL
1 cup	drained fruit cocktail	250 mL
½ cup	raisins	125 mL
½ cup	quartered cherries	125 mL
3 cups	all-purpose flour	750 mL

FRUIT COCKTAIL COOKIES

CONTINUED

Preheat oven to 350°F (180°C). In a large bowl, cream butter and sugar together. Add eggs and beat thoroughly. Stir in vanilla, baking soda, salt and cinnamon. Stir in fruit cocktail, raisins and cherries. Gradually mix in flour. Drop by teaspoonfuls (5 mL) on ungreased cookie sheets. Bake on middle rack for 12-14 minutes.
Makes 4 dozen.

VARIATIONS:

Peach Drops: Substitute drained chopped peaches for fruit cocktail.

BLUEBERRY DROPS

A SOFT CAKE-LIKE COOKIE WITH A SUPER CINNAMON TOPPING.

¾ cup	butter or margarine	175 mL
¾ cup	granulated sugar	175 mL
2	eggs	2
1 tsp.	vanilla	5 mL
2 tsp.	baking powder	10 mL
½ tsp.	salt	2 mL
½ cup	milk	125 mL
1¾ cups	all-purpose flour	425 mL
1½ cups	blueberries (preferably wild ones)	375 mL
3 tbsp.	brown sugar	45 mL
2 tsp.	cinnamon	10 mL

Preheat oven to 350°F (180°C). In a large bowl, cream butter and sugar together. Add eggs and beat thoroughly. Stir in vanilla, baking powder and salt. Alternately mix in milk and flour. Fold in blueberries. Drop by teaspoonfuls (5 mL) on ungreased cookie sheets. Combine cinnamon and sugar to make topping. Sprinkle over cookies. Bake on middle rack for 12-14 minutes.
Makes 3 dozen.

See photograph on page 87.

A P P L E   C O O K I E S

THESE COOKIES HAVE A DELICATE APPLE FLAVOR.

1 cup	butter	250 mL
1 cup	packed brown sugar	250 mL
1	egg	1
1 tsp.	vanilla	5 mL
½ tsp.	baking soda	2 mL
2 tsp.	baking powder	10 mL
1 tsp.	cinnamon	5 mL
½ tsp.	salt	2 mL
2 cups	all-purpose flour	500 mL
1 cup	grated apple	250 mL

Preheat oven to 350°F (180°C). In a large bowl, cream butter and sugar together. Add egg and beat thoroughly. Stir in vanilla, baking soda, baking powder, cinnamon and salt. Gradually mix in flour. Fold in apple. Drop by teaspoonfuls (5 mL) on ungreased cookie sheets. Bake on middle rack for 10-12 minutes. When cool frost with Caramel Icing, if you wish.
Makes 3½ dozen.

CARAMEL ICING

¼ cup	soft butter	60 mL
½ cup	packed brown sugar	125 mL
2 tbsp.	milk	30 mL
¾ cup	icing sugar	175 mL

In a small saucepan, melt butter and brown sugar. Cook on medium heat for 2 minutes. Stir in milk. Cook until mixture boils, stirring constantly. Remove from heat. Cool for about 15 minutes. Stir in icing sugar. Frost cookies when they are cool.

NOTE: To make these cookies without egg, omit egg, increase baking powder to 1 tbsp. (15 mL) and add ⅓ cup (75 mL) sour cream.

See photograph on front cover.

L E M O N D E L I G H T S

THESE COOKIES HAVE A DELICATE LEMON FLAVOR AND ARE ONE OF MY FAVORITES.

¾ cup	butter or margarine	175 mL
¼ cup	granulated sugar	60 mL
½ cup	packed brown sugar	125 mL
1	egg	1
2 tbsp.	grated lemon rind*	30 mL
2 tbsp.	lemon juice	30 mL
½ tsp.	baking soda	2 mL
½ tsp.	baking powder	2 mL
½ tsp.	salt	2 mL
2 cups	all-purpose flour	500 mL

Preheat oven to 375°F (190°C). In a large bowl, cream butter and sugars together. Add egg and beat thoroughly. Stir in lemon rind, lemon juice, baking soda, baking powder and salt. Gradually mix in flour. Form dough into 1" (2.5 cm) balls and place on ungreased cookie sheets. With the tines of a fork which has been dipped in flour, gently press balls into 1½" (4 cm) circles. Sprinkle each circle with granulated sugar. Bake on middle rack for 7-8 minutes.

Makes 5 dozen. These cookies freeze well.

VARIATIONS:

Instead of sprinkling cookies with sugar, sprinkle tops with coconut OR slivered almonds OR place half a pecan on each circle.

* One large lemon will yield the required grated rind and juice for this recipe.

L E M O N C L O U D S

LEMON CLOUDS HAVE A SUPERB TEXTURE AND A DELICATE, UNFORGETTABLE FLAVOR. ONE OF MY FAVORITE COOKIES AND ANOTHER EGGLESS GEM.

½ cup	butter or margarine	125 mL
1 cup	granulated sugar	250 mL
1 cup	sour cream	250 mL
⅓ cup	lemon juice	75 mL
2 tbsp.	grated lemon rind	30 mL
1 tsp.	baking soda	5 mL
1 tsp.	salt	5 mL
½ tsp.	nutmeg	2 mL
2¼ cups	all-purpose flour	550 mL

Preheat oven to 350°F (180°C). In a large bowl, cream butter and sugar together. Stir in sour cream, lemon juice and lemon rind. Mix in baking soda, salt and nutmeg. Gradually mix in flour. Drop by teaspoonfuls (5 mL) on ungreased cookie sheets and bake on middle rack for 10-12 minutes. Allow cookies to cool and then ice with Lemon Frosting.
Makes about 3½ dozen.

LEMON FROSTING

¼ cup	soft butter	60 mL
1 cup	icing sugar	250 mL
2 tsp.	lemon juice	10 mL

In a small bowl, cream butter. Add icing sugar and lemon juice. Beat until smooth and creamy. Ice cooled cookies.

NOTE: These cookies will be very pale when baked.

See photograph on page 35.

Afternoon Tea, clockwise from lower right

Lemon Clouds, page 34
Butter 'N' Sugar Crisps, page 14
Mocha Nut Drops, page 55
Jam Balls, page 58
Rich Dark Fruitcake Cookies, page 48
Berry Muffins, page 78

ORANGE PECAN CRISPS

THESE COOKIES HAVE THE MOST WONDERFUL ORANGE FLAVOR. THEY'RE
ANOTHER OF MY FAVORITES.

¾ cup	butter or margarine	175 mL
¾ cup	granulated sugar	175 mL
1	egg	1
2 tbsp.	grated orange rind*	30 mL
1 tbsp.	orange juice*	15 mL
½ tsp.	baking soda	2 mL
1½ tsp.	baking powder	7 mL
½ tsp.	salt	2 mL
2 cups	all-purpose flour	500 mL
¾ cup	chopped pecans	175 mL

Preheat oven to 375°F (190°C). In a large bowl, cream butter and sugar
together. Add egg and beat thoroughly. Stir in orange rind, orange juice,
baking soda, baking powder and salt. Gradually mix in flour. Fold in
chopped pecans. Form dough into 1" (2.5 cm) balls and place on ungreased
cookie sheets. Using the tines of a fork which has been dipped in flour,
gently press balls into 1½" (4 cm) circles. Bake on middle rack for 8-10
minutes.
Makes 4-4½ dozen. These cookies freeze well.

* One medium orange will provide the rind and juice needed for this recipe.

NOTE: To make these cookies without eggs, omit egg, increase baking
powder to 2 tsp. (10 mL) and add ¼ cup (60 mL) sour cream.

See photograph on page 17.

CRANBERRY COCONUT DROPS

THE TANGY, TART FLAVOR OF CRANBERRIES IS ENHANCED BY ORANGE JUICE AND COCONUT IN THIS COOKIE. BAKE AND ENJOY!

½ cup	butter or margarine	125 mL
1 cup	packed brown sugar	250 mL
2	eggs	2
1½ tsp.	vanilla	7 mL
2 tbsp.	orange juice	30 mL
1 tsp.	salt	5 mL
1 tsp.	baking powder	5 mL
1 tsp.	baking soda	5 mL
2 cups	all-purpose flour	500 mL
1½ cups	chopped cranberries	375 mL
1 cup	shredded coconut	250 mL

Preheat oven to 350°F (180°C). In a large bowl, cream butter and sugar together. Add eggs and beat thoroughly. Stir in vanilla, orange juice, salt, baking powder and baking soda. Gradually mix in flour. Fold in cranberries and coconut. Drop by teaspoonfuls (5 mL) on ungreased cookie sheets. Bake on middle rack for 10-12 minutes.
Makes 3½ dozen.

ORANGE COCONUT BALLS

COCONUT AND ORANGE GIVE THIS COOKIE A GREAT FLAVOR. THESE ARE EASY TO MAKE AND NEVER LAST LONG. ANOTHER NO EGG WONDER.

1 cup	butter or margarine	250 mL
½ cup	granulated sugar	125 mL
1 tsp.	vanilla	5 mL
2 tbsp.	orange juice	30 mL
2 tbsp.	grated orange rind	30 mL
½ tsp.	salt	2 mL
2 cups	all-purpose flour	500 mL
1 cup	coconut	250 mL
½ cup	chopped pecans	125 mL
	orange juice	
	coconut	

ORANGE COCONUT BALLS

CONTINUED

Preheat oven to 350°F (180°C). In a large bowl, cream butter and sugar together. Stir in vanilla, orange juice, orange rind and salt. Gradually work in flour. Fold in coconut and pecans. Form dough into 1" (2.5 cm) balls. Dip balls in orange juice and then roll in coconut. Place on ungreased cookie sheets. Bake on middle rack for 12-15 minutes.
Makes 4 dozen.

ORANGE RAISIN DROPS

THESE ARE SOFT, CAKE-LIKE COOKIES WITH A WONDERFUL ORANGE FLAVOR. THEY'RE A REAL FAVORITE AT OUR HOUSE.

½ cup	butter or margarine	125 mL
1 cup	granulated sugar	250 mL
2	eggs	2
¼ cup	orange juice	60 mL
1 tbsp.	orange rind	15 mL
1 tsp.	baking powder	5 mL
½ tsp.	salt	2 mL
1½ cups	all-purpose flour	375 mL
1 cup	raisins	250 mL

Preheat oven to 375°F (190°C). In a large bowl, cream butter and sugar together. Add eggs and beat thoroughly. Stir in orange juice and rind. Mix in baking powder and salt. Gradually mix in flour. Fold in raisins. Drop by teaspoonfuls (5 mL) on ungreased cookie sheets. Bake on middle rack for 8-10 minutes.
Makes 3 dozen.

See photograph on front cover.

CORNMEAL COOKIES

A CRISP COOKIE THAT IS RICH AND FLAVORFUL. SUPER ANY TIME.

½ cup	butter or margarine	125 mL
¾ cup	granulated sugar	175 mL
1	egg	1
2 tsp.	lemon juice	10 mL
1 tsp.	grated lemon rind	5 mL
1 tsp.	baking powder	5 mL
½ tsp.	salt	2 mL
½ cup	cornmeal	125 mL
1½ cups	all-purpose flour	375 mL
½ cup	raisins	125 mL

Preheat oven to 350°F (180°C). In a large bowl, cream butter and sugar together. Add egg and beat thoroughly. Stir in lemon juice, lemon rind, baking powder, salt and cornmeal. Gradually mix in flour. Stir in raisins. Form dough into 1" (2.5 cm) balls and place on ungreased cookie sheets. Using the tines of a fork which has been dipped in flour, press balls to ⅛" (3 mm) thickness. Bake on middle rack for 9-11 minutes.

Makes about 3 dozen. These cookies freeze well.

S O U R C R E A M R A I S I N D R O P S

A GREAT TASTING COOKIE THAT EVERYONE SEEMS TO ENJOY.

½ cup	butter or margarine	125 mL
1 cup	granulated sugar	250 mL
1	egg	1
½ tsp.	vanilla	2 mL
2 tsp.	grated lemon rind	10 mL
½ tsp.	baking soda	2 mL
½ cup	sour cream	125 mL
1½ cups	all-purpose flour	375 mL
1 cup	raisins	250 mL
1 cup	coconut	250 mL

Preheat oven to 375°F (190°C). In a large bowl, cream butter and sugar together. Add egg and beat thoroughly. Stir in vanilla, lemon rind, baking soda and sour cream. Gradually mix in flour. Fold in raisins and coconut. Drop by teaspoonfuls (5 mL) on ungreased cookie sheets. Bake on middle rack for 10-12 minutes. Frost with Caramel Frosting.
Makes about 3 dozen.

CARAMEL FROSTING II

¼ cup	soft butter	60 mL
½ cup	packed brown sugar	125 mL
2 tbsp.	milk	30 mL
¾ cup	icing sugar	175 mL

In a small saucepan over low heat, melt butter and brown sugar. Cook for 2 minutes. Add milk. Simmer until mixture boils, stirring constantly. Remove from heat. Cool. Add icing sugar. Spread on cooled cookies.

C U R R A N T   C R I S P S

THE COMBINATION OF CURRANTS AND COCONUT IN THESE COOKIES IS
WONDERFUL. A PLEASURE TO MAKE AND A GREATER PLEASURE TO EAT!

¾ cup	butter or margarine	175 mL
1 cup	granulated sugar	250 mL
1	egg	1
1 tsp.	vanilla	5 mL
½ tsp.	baking soda	2 mL
½ tsp.	salt	2 mL
2 cups	all-purpose flour	500 mL
¾ cup	coconut	175 mL
¾ cup	currants	175 mL

Preheat oven to 375°F (190°C). In a large bowl, cream butter and sugar
together. Add egg and beat thoroughly. Stir in vanilla, baking soda and salt.
Gradually mix in flour. Stir in coconut and currants. Form dough into 1"
(2.5 cm) balls and place on ungreased cookie sheets. With the bottom of a
glass dipped in flour, flatten to ⅛" (3 mm) thickness. Bake on middle rack
for 6-8 minutes. When cookies are cool, ice with Vanilla Frosting.
Makes about 4 dozen.

VANILLA FROSTING II

1½ cups	icing sugar	375 mL
1 tsp.	vanilla	5 mL
¼ cup	soft butter	60 mL
1 tbsp.	lemon juice	15 mL
4	drops yellow food coloring	4

In a small bowl, cream all ingredients together until smooth and creamy.
Spread on cooled cookies.

C U R R A N T D R O P S

CURRANTS WERE ONE OF MY GRANDMA'S FAVORITE FOODS AND I ALSO LIKE THEIR DISTINCTIVE FLAVOR. THIS IS A GREAT RECIPE FOR CURRANT LOVERS.

1 cup	butter or margarine	250 mL
½ cup	granulated sugar	125 mL
½ cup	packed brown sugar	125 mL
2	eggs	2
1 tsp.	lemon extract	5 mL
½ tsp.	baking soda	2 mL
¼ tsp.	salt	1 mL
1¾ cups	all-purpose flour	425 mL
2 cups	currants	500 mL

Preheat oven to 350°F (180°C). In a large bowl, cream butter and sugars together. Add eggs and beat thoroughly. Stir in lemon extract, baking soda and salt. Gradually mix in flour. Fold in currants. Drop by teaspoonfuls (5 mL) on ungreased cookie sheets. Bake on middle rack for 10-12 minutes. **Makes 4 dozen. These cookies freeze well.**

D A T E   A N D   N U T   C O O K I E S

A GREAT COOKIE FOR BREAKFAST OR COFFEE BREAK. THIS COOKIE TRAVELS WELL IN LUNCH BOXES AND IS A GOOD AFTER-SCHOOL SNACK TOO.

1 cup	butter or margarine	250 mL
½ cup	granulated sugar	125 mL
½ cup	packed brown sugar	125 mL
3	eggs	3
1 tsp.	vanilla	5 mL
1 tsp.	baking soda	5 mL
½ tsp.	salt	2 mL
1 tsp.	cinnamon	5 mL
2 cups	all-purpose flour	500 mL
½ lb.	dates, chopped	250 g
1 cup	chopped filberts	250 mL

Preheat oven to 350°F (180°C). In a large bowl, cream butter and sugars together. Add eggs and beat thoroughly. Stir in vanilla, baking soda, salt and cinnamon. Gradually mix in flour. Fold in dates and filberts. Drop by teaspoonfuls (5 mL) on ungreased cookie sheets. Bake on middle rack for 10-12 minutes.
Makes about 6 dozen.

P I N E A P P L E   D A T E   D R O P S

A FLAVORFUL CHEWY COOKIE. GREAT FOR LUNCH BOXES OR SNACKS.

½ cup	butter or margarine	125 mL
¾ cup	packed brown sugar	175 mL
1	egg	1
1 tbsp.	pineapple juice	15 mL
¾ cup	drained, crushed pineapple	175 mL
½ tsp.	vanilla	2 mL
1 tsp.	baking powder	5 mL
½ tsp.	baking soda	2 mL
¼ tsp.	salt	1 mL
2 cups	all-purpose flour	500 mL
1 cup	chopped dates	250 mL

P I N E A P P L E   D A T E   D R O P S

CONTINUED

Preheat oven to 375°F (190°C). In a large bowl, cream butter and brown sugar. Add egg and beat thoroughly. Stir in pineapple juice, pineapple, vanilla, baking powder, baking soda and salt. Gradually mix in flour. Fold in dates. Drop by teaspoonfuls (5 mL) on ungreased cookie sheets. Bake on middle rack for 12-15 minutes.
Makes about 3 dozen.

P I N E A P P L E   C O C O N U T   D R O P S

PINEAPPLE AND COCONUT CREATE A SOFT, CAKE-LIKE COOKIE.

½ cup	butter or margarine	125 mL
¾ cup	granulated sugar	175 mL
1	egg	1
¾ cup	drained, crushed pineapple	175 mL
1 tbsp.	pineapple juice, from pineapple	15 mL
½ tsp.	vanilla	2 mL
½ tsp.	baking soda	2 mL
1 tsp.	baking powder	5 mL
¼ tsp.	salt	1 mL
2 cups	all-purpose flour	500 mL
¾ cups	sweet, flaked coconut	175 mL

Preheat oven to 375°F (190°C). In a large bowl, cream butter and sugar. Add egg and beat thoroughly. Stir in crushed pineapple, pineapple juice, and vanilla. Stir in baking soda, baking powder and salt. Gradually mix in flour. Fold in coconut. Drop by teaspoonfuls (5 mL) on ungreased cookie sheets. Bake on middle rack for 10-12 minutes or until tops of cookies are golden brown.
Makes 3½-4 dozen.

C H E R R Y   N U T   C O O K I E S

A COLORFUL COOKIE, WONDERFUL FOR CHRISTMAS AND YEAR-ROUND.

½ cup	butter	125 mL
¼ cup	granulated sugar	60 mL
1	egg	1
1 tsp.	vanilla	5 mL
1 tsp.	almond extract	5 mL
½ tsp.	salt	2 mL
1 cup	all-purpose flour	250 mL
½ cup	chopped pecans	125 mL
	cherries	

Preheat oven to 375°F (190°C). In a large bowl, cream butter and sugar together. Add egg and beat thoroughly. Stir in vanilla, almond extract and salt. Gradually mix in flour. Form dough into 1" (2.5 cm) balls. Roll balls in chopped pecans. Place on ungreased cookie sheets and flatten slightly with finger. Place ½ a cherry on top of each ball. Bake on middle rack 15-20 minutes.
Makes 3 dozen.

CHERRY ICE BOX COOKIES

THIS IS AN EASY COOKIE TO MAKE AND HANDY TO HAVE IN THE FREEZER IF UNEXPECTED COMPANY ARRIVES. A PRETTY COOKIE, AS THE CHERRIES GIVE IT A PALE PINK COLOR. GREAT FOR CHRISTMAS TOO!

1 cup	butter or margarine	250 mL
1 cup	granulated sugar	250 mL
2	eggs	2
1 tsp.	almond extract	5 mL
½ tsp.	vanilla	2 mL
2 tsp.	baking powder	10 mL
1 tsp.	salt	5 mL
2¾ cups	all-purpose flour	675 mL
1 cup	finely chopped cherries	250 mL

In a large bowl, cream butter and sugar together. Add eggs and beat thoroughly. Stir in almond extract, vanilla, baking powder and salt. Gradually mix in flour. Fold in cherries. Divide dough in ½. Form each ½ into a long roll. Wrap in plastic wrap and refrigerate for at least 1 hour. When ready to bake, preheat oven to 400°F (200°C). Cut rolls into slices and place on ungreased cookie sheets. The thinner the slices the crispier the cookie and the less time needed to bake. For ¼" (1 cm) thick slices, bake 8-10 minutes. For thicker slices bake 10-12 minutes.

Makes 7 dozen. These cookies freeze well.

RICH, DARK FRUIT CAKE COOKIES

I ESPECIALLY LIKE FRUIT CAKE AND ADAPTED MY RECIPE, SO I COULD MAKE COOKIES WITH IT. NOW I CAN HAVE FRUIT CAKE COOKIES AT ANY TIME OF THE YEAR, NOT JUST AT CHRISTMAS.

½ cup	butter	125 mL
½ cup	packed brown sugar	125 mL
2	eggs	2
½ cup	molasses	125 mL
¼ cup	sour cream	60 mL
½ tsp.	baking soda	2 mL
¼ tsp.	cloves	1 mL
¼ tsp.	allspice	1 mL
¼ tsp.	nutmeg	1 mL
¼ tsp.	cinnamon	1 mL
1 tsp.	cocoa	5 mL
¼ tsp.	salt	1 mL
½ tsp.	vanilla	2 mL
½ tsp.	rum extract	2 mL
½ tsp.	lemon extract	2 mL
¼ cup	pure strawberry jam	60 mL
3 cups	all-purpose flour	750 mL
¾ cup	raisins	175 mL
½ cup	currants	125 mL
½ cup	mixed fruit peel	125 mL
7½ oz.	pkg. mixed red and green glazed cherries, halved	225 g
¼ cup	halved red maraschino cherries	60 mL
¼ cup	halved green maraschino cherries	60 mL
½ cup	chopped dates	125 mL
½ cup	slivered almonds	125 mL

RICH, DARK FRUIT CAKE COOKIES

CONTINUED

Preheat oven to 350°F (180°C). In a very large bowl, cream butter and sugar together. Add eggs and beat thoroughly. Stir in molasses. In a separate bowl, stir baking soda into sour cream. Stir into butter mixture. Mix in spices, cocoa, salt, vanilla, rum extract, lemon extract and strawberry jam. Gradually mix in flour. Fold in raisins, currants, mixed peel, cherries, dates and almonds. Drop by teaspoonfuls (5 mL) on ungreased cookie sheets. Bake on middle rack for 10-12 minutes.

Makes 4 dozen. These cookies freeze well.

See photograph on page 35.

MIXED FRUIT PEEL COOKIES

THESE COOKIES ARE SOFT, RICH AND VERY COLORFUL.

1 cup	butter	250 mL
½ cup	granulated sugar	125 mL
½ cup	packed brown sugar	125 mL
2	eggs	2
½ tsp.	vanilla	2 mL
1 tsp.	baking soda	5 mL
½ tsp.	cream of tartar	2 mL
½ tsp.	salt	2 mL
1½ cups	all-purpose flour	375 mL
1½ cups	mixed fruit peel	375 mL

Preheat oven to 375°F (190°C). In a large bowl, cream butter and sugars together. Add eggs and beat thoroughly. Stir in vanilla, baking soda, cream of tartar and salt. Gradually add flour, mixing well. Fold in fruit peel. Drop by teaspoonfuls (5 mL) on ungreased cookie sheets. Allow at least 2" (5 cm) between each cookie as they spread out quite a bit. Bake on middle rack for 9-11 minutes.

Makes 3 dozen. These cookies freeze well.

LIGHT FRUIT CAKE COOKIES

A WONDERFUL COOKIE TO MAKE AROUND CHRISTMAS TIME BUT ONE THAT'S A FAVORITE ALL YEAR ROUND. THIS IS A VERY PRETTY COOKIE WITH GREAT TASTE. THESE COOKIES CAN BE MADE WITH MARGARINE BUT BUTTER IS RECOMMENDED FOR ITS RICHER FLAVOR.

1 cup	butter	250 mL
1 cup	granulated sugar	250 mL
3	eggs	3
1½ tsp.	vanilla	7 mL
1 tbsp.	baking powder	15 mL
1 tsp.	salt	5 mL
1 cup	milk	250 mL
3 cups	all-purpose flour	750 mL
1 cup	raisins	250 mL
¾ cup	currants	175 mL
1 cup	mixed fruit peel	250 mL
1 cup	quartered, red and green glazed cherries	250 mL

Preheat oven to 350°F (180°C). In a large bowl, cream butter and sugar together. Add eggs and beat thoroughly. Stir in vanilla, baking powder and salt. Alternately mix in milk and flour. Fold in raisins, currants, fruit peel and cherries. Drop by teaspoonfuls (5 mL) on ungreased cookie sheets. Bake on middle rack for 12-15 minutes.

Makes about 5½ dozen. These cookies freeze well.

See photograph on the back cover.

CHOCOLATE · COOKIES

CHOCOLATE CHIPS SUPREME

THIS IS MY DAUGHTER'S ALL-TIME FAVORITE COOKIE. WE MUST HAVE MADE THOUSANDS OF THESE OVER THE YEARS. THEY'RE A SOFT COOKIE AND THE HONEY ADDS A SUPERB FLAVOR TO THE CHOCOLATE CHIPS.

½ cup	butter or margarine	125 mL
⅓ cup	packed brown sugar	75 mL
⅓ cup	soft honey	75 mL
1	egg	1
½ tsp.	vanilla	2 mL
½ tsp.	baking soda	2 mL
½ tsp.	salt	2 mL
1 cup+2 tbsp.	all-purpose flour	275 mL
6 oz.	pkg. semisweet chocolate chips	175 g

Preheat oven to 375°F (190°C). In a large bowl, cream butter and sugar together. Stir in honey. Add egg and beat thoroughly. Stir in vanilla, baking soda and salt. Gradually mix in flour. Fold in chocolate chips. Drop by teaspoonfuls (5 mL) on ungreased cookie sheets. Bake on middle rack for 10-12 minutes.

Makes 3½ dozen. These cookies freeze well.

VARIATION:

Omit the chocolate chips and substitute 1 cup (250 mL) butterscotch chips.

See photograph on front cover.

C H O C O L A T E   D R O P S

EXQUISITE TASTE WITH DOUBLE THE CHOCOLATE FLAVOR. SO SIMPLE TO
MAKE AND DELICIOUS TO EAT. THIS IS A SOFT, CAKE-LIKE COOKIE WHICH
SIMPLY DISAPPEARS AS SOON AS IT'S IN THE COOKIE JAR.

¼ cup	shortening	60 mL
½ cup	packed brown sugar	125 mL
½ cup	soft honey	125 mL
1	egg	1
1 tsp.	vanilla	5 mL
½ cup	cocoa or 2 squares, 2 oz. (55 g) melted	125 mL
	unsweetened chocolate	
½ tsp.	baking soda	2 mL
1 tsp.	salt	5 mL
½ cup	sour milk (see page 20)	125 mL
2 cups	all-purpose flour	500 mL

Preheat oven to 350°F (180°C). In a large bowl, cream shortening and
brown sugar together. Add honey and mix well. Add egg and beat
thoroughly. Stir in vanilla, cocoa, baking soda and salt. Alternately mix in
sour milk and flour. Drop by teaspoonfuls (5 mL) on ungreased cookie sheets
and bake on middle rack for 10-12 minutes. Once cookies are cool, frost
with Chocolate Icing.
Makes 3 dozen.

CHOCOLATE ICING II

1¼ cups	icing sugar	300 mL
2 tbsp.	cocoa	30 mL
⅛ tsp.	salt	0.5 mL
2 tbsp.	soft butter	30 mL
2 tbsp.	milk	30 mL

In a small bowl, combine icing sugar, cocoa and salt. Mix in butter. Stir in
milk and continue to stir until mixture is smooth and creamy. Spread
mixture over cookies.

See photograph on the back cover.

CHOCOLATE MINT DELIGHTS

ANYONE WHO LIKES THE COMBINATION OF CHOCOLATE AND PEPPERMINT WILL LOVE THESE COOKIES. THEY'RE ABSOLUTELY DELICIOUS.

1 cup	butter	250 mL
1 cup	granulated sugar	250 mL
2	eggs	2
½ tsp.	vanilla	2 mL
1 tsp.	baking soda	5 mL
½ tsp.	cream of tartar	2 mL
½ tsp.	salt	2 mL
½ cup	cocoa	125 mL
2½ cups	all-purpose flour	625 mL

Preheat oven to 375°F (190°C). In a large bowl, cream butter and sugar together. Add eggs and beat thoroughly. Stir in vanilla, baking soda, cream of tartar, salt and cocoa. Gradually mix in flour. Form dough into 1" (2.5 cm) balls and place on ungreased cookie sheets. Using the tines of a fork which has been dipped in flour, gently press balls into 1½" (4 cm) circles. Bake on middle rack for 5-6 minutes. When cookies are cool, frost with Mint Icing. **Makes about 5 dozen.**

MINT ICING

½ cup	soft butter	125 mL
1½ cups	icing sugar	375 mL
2 tsp.	peppermint extract	10 mL
5-6	drops green food coloring	5-6

In a small bowl, cream butter and icing sugar together. Stir in peppermint extract and food coloring. Spread on cooled cookies.

M O C H A   N U T   D R O P S

A RICH, MOCHA COOKIE WITH SUPERB FLAVOR. EASY TO MAKE.

½ cup	butter or margarine	125 mL
1 cup	packed brown sugar	250 mL
¼ cup	soft honey	60 mL
2	eggs	2
1 tsp.	vanilla	5 mL
½ cup	cocoa	125 mL
½ tsp.	baking soda	2 mL
¼ tsp.	salt	1 mL
2 tsp.	instant coffee	10 mL
½ cup	sour milk (see page 20)	125 mL
2 cups	all-purpose flour	500 mL
1 cup	chopped pecans	250 mL
	finely chopped pecans	

Preheat oven to 375°F (190°C). In a large bowl, cream butter and sugar together. Stir in honey. Add eggs and beat thoroughly. Stir in vanilla, cocoa, baking soda, salt and instant coffee. Alternately mix in sour milk and flour. Fold in nuts. Drop by teaspoonfuls on ungreased cookie sheets. Bake on middle rack for 10-12 minutes. When cookies are cool, frost with Mocha Frosting and sprinkle with finely chopped pecans.
Makes 3 dozen.

MOCHA FROSTING

½ cup	butter	125 mL
2 tbsp.	cocoa	30 mL
2 tsp.	instant coffee	10 mL
1 tsp.	vanilla	5 mL
2 cups	icing sugar	500 mL
1 tbsp.	milk	15 mL

In a small bowl, cream butter. Add cocoa, instant coffee and vanilla. Stir until smooth. Gradually mix in icing sugar and milk, until mixture is creamy. Spread on cooled cookies.

See photograph on page 35.

❖ ❖ ❖ ❖ ❖ ❖

CHOCOLATE PEANUT CRISPS

EVERYONE LOVES THESE VERY CRISP FLAVORFUL COOKIES.

½ cup	butter	125 mL
1½ cups	packed brown sugar	375 mL
1	egg	1
1 tsp.	vanilla	5 mL
½ tsp.	each baking soda and salt	2 mL
1½ cups	all-purpose flour	375 mL
1 cup	baking peanuts	250 mL
3x1 oz.	squares semisweet chocolate, melted	3x30 g

Preheat oven to 375°F (190°C). In a large bowl, cream butter and brown sugar together. Add egg and beat thoroughly. Stir in vanilla, baking soda and salt. Gradually mix in flour. Form dough into 1" (2.5 cm) balls and place on ungreased cookie sheets. Using the tines of a fork which has been dipped in flour, gently press balls into small circles. Place peanut halves on top of circles. Bake on middle rack for 8-10 minutes. Place on racks to cool. Once cookies are cooled, melt chocolate squares and drizzle the chocolate over the cookies.
Makes 5 dozen.

PEANUTTY CHOCOLATE BALLS

AN EASY-TO-MAKE, NO-BAKE COOKIE THAT KIDS JUST LOVE.

¾ cup	sweetened, condensed milk	175 mL
½ cup	chocolate chips	125 mL
½ cup	butterscotch chips	125 mL
1 cup	peanuts	250 mL
1½ cups	graham wafer crumbs	375 mL
	coconut	

In a 3-quart (3 L) saucepan, over low heat, melt milk, chocolate chips and butterscotch chips. Stir in peanuts and graham wafer crumbs. Mix thoroughly. Form mixture into 1" (2.5 cm) balls. Roll balls in coconut. Place in Petit Four cups, see page 58.
Makes about 2½ dozen.

See photograph on page 17.

R U M B A L L S

THESE ARE A GREAT FAVORITE AT CHRISTMAS. THIS IS A FAMILY SPECIALTY.

¼ cup	melted butter	60 mL
¼ cup	white rum	60 mL
2 tbsp.	corn syrup	30 mL
1 tbsp.	milk	15 mL
2 cups	graham wafer crumbs	500 mL
1½ cups	icing sugar	375 mL
48	maraschino cherry halves	48
	chocolate sprinkles	

In a medium-sized saucepan, over low heat, melt butter. Stir in rum, corn syrup and milk. Mix in graham wafer crumbs and icing sugar. Grease hands well with butter. Break off about 1½ tsp. (7 mL) of the dough. Flatten slightly, using the palm of your hand. Lay ½ a cherry on the flattened mixture. Shape into a ball, with the ½ cherry in the centre. Roll in chocolate sprinkles. Place in Petit Four cups, see page 58.
Makes about 4 dozen.

NOTE: If your hands get sticky, you may need to wash them and regrease with butter.

COCONUT GRAHAM BALLS

A QUICK AND EASY TREAT TO MAKE. ANOTHER GREAT NO EGG RECIPE.

¾ cup	sweetened, condensed milk	175 mL
½ cup	chocolate chips	125 mL
1 cup	chopped nuts, of your choice	250 mL
1¼ cups	graham wafer crumbs	300 mL
	coconut	

In a small saucepan, over low heat, stir the milk and chocolate chips until smooth and all chips are melted. Remove from heat. Stir in nuts and graham wafer crumbs. Shape mixture into 1" (2.5 cm) balls. Roll balls in coconut. **Makes about 3 dozen.**

JAM BALLS

THIS IS A SUPER, EASY-TO-MAKE, NO-BAKE COOKIE. IT'S A GREAT TREAT AT ANY TIME OF YEAR, BUT IS ALSO A PARTICULARLY GOOD CHRISTMAS COOKIE.

¾ cup	raspberry jam	175 mL
3 tbsp.	butter	45 mL
1 tsp.	vanilla	5 mL
2¼ cups	graham wafer crumbs	550 mL
	chocolate sprinkles	

In a 3-quart (3 L) saucepan, on low heat, combine the jam and butter. Stir until the butter is melted. Remove from heat. Add vanilla and crumbs. Mix thoroughly. Form mixture into 1" (2.5 cm) balls. Roll balls in chocolate sprinkles. Place in Petit Four cups. These paper cups can be purchased at most kitchen shops.
Makes about 2½ dozen.

See photograph on page 35.

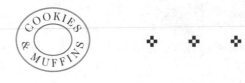

A P P L E S A U C E   G E M S

FOR OLD-FASHIONED GOODNESS, YOU CAN'T BEAT THIS APPLESAUCE COOKIE. THE ROLLED OATS GIVES IT A HEALTHY DIMENSION AND THE TASTE IS SUPERB.

½ cup	butter or margarine	125 mL
1 cup	packed brown sugar	250 mL
2	eggs	2
1 tsp.	vanilla	5 mL
1 tsp.	baking soda	5 mL
1 cup	applesauce	250 mL
½ tsp.	salt	2 mL
1 tsp.	cinnamon	5 mL
2½ cups	all-purpose flour	625 mL
1½ cups	rolled oats	375 mL

Preheat oven to 350°F (180°C). In a large bowl, cream butter and brown sugar together. Add eggs and beat thoroughly. Stir in vanilla. In a separate bowl, mix baking soda with applesauce. (The soda will make the applesauce fizz a bit.) Stir the baking soda and applesauce mixture into the butter mixture. Stir in cinnamon. Gradually add flour. Fold in the rolled oats. Drop by teaspoonfuls (5 mL) on ungreased cookie sheets. Bake on middle rack for 12-14 minutes.
Makes 3½ dozen. These cookies freeze well.

S M A R T I E   C O O K I E S

ANOTHER RECIPE WITH NO EGGS. THESE ARE MOIST AND CAKE-LIKE.

½ cup	butter or margarine	125 mL
1 cup	packed brown sugar	250 mL
2 tsp.	baking soda	10 mL
1½ cups	applesauce	375 mL
½ tsp.	salt	2 mL
1½ cups	rolled oats	375 mL
2½ cups	all-purpose flour	625 mL
1 cup	Smarties	250 mL

SMARTIE COOKIES

CONTINUED

Preheat oven to 350°F (180°C). In a large bowl, cream butter and sugar together. In a separate bowl, stir the baking soda into applesauce. (This will cause the applesauce to fizz.) Stir into butter mixture. Stir in salt and rolled oats. Gradually mix in flour. Fold in Smarties. Drop by teaspoonfuls (5 mL) on ungreased cookie sheets. Bake on middle rack for 10-12 minutes.
Makes 3 dozen.

CHOCOLATE OATMEAL GEMS

THESE COOKIES PROVIDE FIBER-RICH OATMEAL AS WELL AS HONEY AND NUTS. GREAT FOR LUNCH BOXES OR AFTER-SCHOOL SNACKS.

1 cup	butter or margarine	250 mL
1 cup	packed brown sugar	250 mL
½ cup	soft honey	125 mL
2	eggs	2
1 tsp.	vanilla	5 mL
½ tsp.	baking soda	2 mL
1 tsp.	salt	5 mL
2 cups	all-purpose flour	500 mL
2 cups	rolled oats	500 mL
6 oz.	pkg. chocolate chips	175 g
1 cup	chopped Brazil nuts	250 mL

Preheat oven to 350°F (180°C). In a large bowl, cream butter and sugar together. Stir in honey. Add eggs and beat thoroughly. Stir in vanilla, baking soda and salt. Gradually mix in flour. Stir in rolled oats. Fold in chocolate chips and nuts. Drop by teaspoonfuls (5 mL) on ungreased cookie sheets. Bake on middle rack for 10-12 minutes.
Makes 4 dozen.

CHOCOLATE COCONUT MACAROONS

Kids love these and they're so easy to make — no baking necessary.

1½ cups	granulated sugar	375 mL
5 tbsp.	cocoa	75 mL
½ cup	milk	125 mL
½ cup	butter or margarine	125 mL
1 tsp.	vanilla	5 mL
1 cup	shredded coconut	250 mL
3½ cups	rolled oats	875 mL

In a 4-quart (4 L) saucepan, combine sugar and cocoa working out any lumps, mix thoroughly. Slowly add milk, stirring well. Add butter. Place saucepan on medium heat. Bring mixture to a boil while stirring constantly. Remove from heat. Stir in vanilla and coconut. Fold in rolled oats. Drop by teaspoonfuls (5 mL) on wax paper. Chill in refrigerator until firm.
Makes 4 dozen.

GUM DROP COOKIES

A real treat for adults and children alike. The gum drops give these cookies a unique flavor and the cookies never last long.

1 cup	butter or margarine	250 mL
1 cup	packed brown sugar	250 mL
¼ cup	granulated sugar	60 mL
2	eggs	2
1 tsp.	vanilla	5 mL
1 tsp.	baking powder	5 mL
½ tsp.	baking soda	2 mL
½ tsp.	salt	2 mL
1½ cups	all-purpose flour	375 mL
1 cup	rolled oats	250 mL
1 cup	finely chopped gum drops (don't use black)	250 mL
1 cup	slivered almonds	250 mL

GUM DROP COOKIES

CONTINUED

Preheat oven to 350°F (180°C). In a large bowl, cream butter and sugars together. Add eggs and beat thoroughly. Stir in vanilla, baking powder, baking soda and salt. Gradually mix in flour. Fold in rolled oats, gum drops, and almonds. Drop by teaspoonfuls (5 mL) on ungreased cookie sheets. Bake on middle rack for 10-12 minutes.
Makes 4 dozen.

See photograph on page 69.

BANANA ALMOND OATS

THIS COOKIE HAS A WONDERFULLY RICH AND SATISFYING FLAVOR. SIMPLY DELICIOUS, THESE ARE GREAT FOR BREAKFAST, LUNCH, OR JUST ANY TIME.

¾ cup	butter or margarine	175 mL
1 cup	granulated sugar	250 mL
1	egg	1
1	large, ripe banana, mashed	1
½ tsp.	lemon juice	2 mL
½ tsp.	baking soda	2 mL
½ tsp.	salt	2 mL
¾ tsp.	cinnamon	3 mL
¼ tsp.	nutmeg	1 mL
1½ cups	all-purpose flour	375 mL
1½ cups	rolled oats	375 mL
1 cup	slivered almonds	250 mL

Preheat oven to 350°F (180°C). In a large bowl, cream butter and sugar together. Add egg and beat thoroughly. Stir in banana and lemon juice. Add baking soda, salt, cinnamon and nutmeg. Gradually mix in flour. Fold in rolled oats and almonds. Drop by teaspoonfuls (5 mL) on ungreased cookie sheets. Bake on middle rack for 12-15 minutes.
Makes 4 dozen. These cookies freeze well.

A P R I C O T   G E M S

THE DRIED APRICOTS GIVE THIS COOKIE A GREAT FLAVOR.

1 cup	butter or margarine	250 mL
1 cup	packed brown sugar	250 mL
2	eggs	2
1 tsp.	vanilla	5 mL
1 tsp.	baking soda	5 mL
½ tsp.	salt	2 mL
1½ cups	all-purpose flour	375 mL
1½ cups	rolled oats	375 mL
1 cup	finely chopped dried apricots	250 mL
1 cup	chopped pecans	250 mL

Preheat oven to 350°F (180°C). In a large bowl, cream butter and sugar together. Add eggs and beat thoroughly. Stir in vanilla, baking soda and salt. Gradually mix in flour. Fold in rolled oats, apricots and pecans. Drop by teaspoonfuls (5 mL) on ungreased cookie sheets. Bake on middle rack for 12-15 minutes.
Makes 4 dozen.

P E A C H   ' N '   A L M O N D   C L U S T E R S

A WHOLESOME COOKIE FOR LUNCHES OR AFTER-SCHOOL SNACKS.

1 cup	butter or margarine	250 mL
½ cup	granulated sugar	125 mL
½ cup	packed brown sugar	125 mL
2	eggs	2
½ tsp.	vanilla	2 mL
½ tsp.	almond extract	2 mL
1 tsp.	baking soda	5 mL
½ tsp.	salt	2 mL
1½ cups	all-purpose flour	375 mL
1½ cups	rolled oats	375 mL
1 cup	finely chopped dried peaches	250 mL
1 cup	slivered almonds	250 mL

PEACH 'N' ALMOND CLUSTERS

CONTINUED

Preheat oven to 350°F (180°C). In a large bowl, cream butter and sugars together. Add eggs and beat thoroughly. Stir in vanilla, almond extract, baking soda and salt. Gradually mix in flour. Fold in rolled oats, peaches and almonds. Drop by teaspoonfuls (5 mL) on ungreased cookie sheets. Bake on middle rack for 12-14 minutes.
Makes 4 dozen.

MIXED FRUIT AND NUT CLUSTERS

A GREAT BREAKFAST AND SNACK COOKIE!

½ cup	butter or margarine	125 mL
½ cup	packed brown sugar	125 mL
½ cup	soft honey	125 mL
1	egg	1
½ tsp.	vanilla	2 mL
1 tsp.	lemon extract	5 mL
½ tsp.	baking soda	2 mL
½ tsp.	salt	2 mL
1 tsp.	cinnamon	5 mL
½ tsp.	allspice	2 mL
1½ cups	all-purpose flour	375 mL
1¼ cups	rolled oats	300 mL
2 cups	chopped, mixed dried fruit	500 mL
1 cup	flaked filberts	250 mL

Preheat oven to 375°F (190°C). In a large bowl, cream butter and sugar together. Stir in honey, add egg and beat thoroughly. Stir in vanilla, lemon extract, baking soda, salt, cinnamon and allspice. Gradually mix in flour. Fold in rolled oats, dried fruit and filberts. Drop by teaspoonfuls (5 mL) on ungreased cookie sheets. Bake on middle rack for 8-10 minutes.
Makes 4 dozen.

See photograph on page 69.

C O R N F L A K E   C O O K I E S

ANOTHER GREAT BREAKFAST COOKIE. SUPER SERVED WITH JAM OR
MARMALADE.

1 cup	butter or margarine	250 mL
½ cup	granulated sugar	125 mL
½ cup	packed brown sugar	125 mL
1	egg	1
1 tsp.	vanilla	5 mL
½ tsp.	baking powder	2 mL
¼ tsp.	baking soda	1 mL
½ tsp.	salt	2 mL
1 tsp.	cinnamon	5 mL
½ tsp.	allspice	2 mL
1½ cups	all-purpose flour	375 mL
¾ cup	rolled oats	175 mL
1¾ cups	cornflakes	425 mL

Preheat oven to 350°F (180°C). In a large bowl, cream butter and sugars
together. Add egg and beat thoroughly. Stir in vanilla, baking powder, baking
soda, salt, cinnamon and allspice. Gradually mix in flour. Fold in rolled oats
and cornflakes. Drop by teaspoonfuls (5 mL) on ungreased cookie sheets.
Bake on middle rack for 10-12 minutes.
Makes 3½ dozen. These cookies freeze well.

VARIATION:

Add ¾ cup (175 mL) raisins or nuts of your choice if desired.

NOTE: To make these cookies without eggs, omit egg, increase baking
powder to 2 tsp. (10 mL) and add ¼ cup (60 mL) sour cream or yogurt.

HONEY 'N' ALMOND GEMS

THESE WONDERFULLY SPICY COOKIES ARE ABSOLUTELY DELICIOUS. EVERYONE LOVES THEM AND HONEY, ROLLED OATS AND ALMONDS MAKE THEM A HEALTHY SNACK.

1 cup	butter or margarine	250 mL
½ cup	packed brown sugar	125 mL
½ cup	soft honey	125 mL
2	eggs	2
1 tsp.	vanilla	5 mL
1 tsp.	baking soda	5 mL
1 tsp.	salt	5 mL
1 tsp.	cinnamon	5 mL
½ tsp.	nutmeg	2 mL
½ tsp.	cloves	2 mL
1½ cups	all-purpose flour	375 mL
1½ cups	rolled oats	375 mL
1 cup	slivered almonds	250 mL

Preheat oven to 375°F (190°C). In a large bowl, cream butter and sugar together. Stir in honey. Add eggs and beat thoroughly. Stir in vanilla, baking soda, salt and spices. Gradually mix in flour. Fold in rolled oats and almonds. Drop by teaspoonfuls (5 mL) on ungreased cookie sheets. Bake on middle rack for 10-12 minutes.

Makes 4 dozen. These cookies freeze well.

VARIATION:

Honey 'N' Raisin Gems: Add 1 cup (250 mL) of raisins to this recipe instead of the almonds.

R A I S I N   B R A N   G E M S

TRY THESE COOKIES WITH JAM OR MARMALADE.

¾ cup	butter	175 mL
1½ cups	packed brown sugar	375 mL
2	eggs	2
1½ tsp.	vanilla	7 mL
1 tsp.	baking powder	5 mL
½ tsp.	baking soda	2 mL
1½ tsp.	cinnamon	7 mL
1 tsp.	salt	5 mL
1½ cups	all-purpose flour	375 mL
1 cup	bran flakes	250 mL
¾ cup	raisins	175 mL
¾ cup	flaked brazil nuts	175 mL

Preheat oven to 350°F (180°C). In a large bowl, cream butter and brown sugar together. Add eggs and beat thoroughly. Stir in vanilla, baking powder, baking soda, cinnamon and salt. Gradually mix in flour. Fold in bran flakes, raisins and brazil nuts. Drop by teaspoonfuls (5 mL) on ungreased cookie sheets and bake on middle rack for 10-12 minutes.
Makes 4 dozen. These cookies freeze well.

VARIATION:

Raisin Oatmeal Gems: Substitute 1 cup (250 mL) of rolled oats for the bran flakes.

Lunch Time, clockwise from lower right

Gum Drop Cookies, page 62
Mixed Fruit and Nut Clusters, page 65
Spicy Carrot Muffins, page 95
Peanut Butter Cookies, page 21

ORANGE 'N' BRAN MARMALADE GEMS

A GREAT BREAKFAST COOKIE WITH BRAN, ALMONDS AND MARMALADE. CHILDREN LOVE THEM AND DON'T EVEN REALIZE THEY'RE ALSO EATING LOTS OF FIBER.

1 cup	bran flakes	250 mL
2 tbsp.	orange juice *	30 mL
2 tbsp.	grated orange rind *	30 mL
¾ cup	sour cream	175 mL
½ cup	butter or margarine	125 mL
1 cup	granulated sugar	250 mL
1	egg	1
½ tsp.	baking soda	2 mL
½ tsp.	salt	2 mL
1½ cups	all-purpose flour	375 mL
1 cup	chopped almonds	250 mL
	marmalade for topping	

Preheat oven to 350°F (180°C). Combine bran flakes, orange juice, orange rind and sour cream. Set aside. In a separate bowl, cream butter and sugar. Add egg and beat thoroughly. Stir in bran flake mixture. Stir in baking soda and salt. Gradually mix in flour. Fold in almonds. Drop by teaspoonfuls (5 mL) on ungreased cookie sheets and bake on middle rack for 12-14 minutes. Frost cookies with marmalade while they are still warm.
Makes 4 dozen.

* One large orange will yield the required grated rind and juice for this recipe.

See photograph on page 87.

O R A N G E B R A N C O O K I E S

A GREAT BREAKFAST OR COFFEE BREAK COOKIE WITH LOTS OF FIBER AND VITAMINS. HEALTHY AND DELICIOUS!

¾ cup	butter or margarine	175 mL
¾ cup	granulated sugar	175 mL
2	eggs	2
½ tsp.	vanilla	2 mL
3 tbsp.	orange juice	45 mL
2 tbsp.	grated orange rind	30 mL
1½ tsp.	baking powder	7 mL
¾ tsp.	salt	3 mL
1½ cups	all-purpose flour	375 mL
1¼ cups	bran flakes cereal	300 mL
1 cup	chocolate chips	250 mL

Preheat oven to 350°F (180°C). In a large bowl, cream butter and sugar together. Add eggs and beat thoroughly. Stir in vanilla, orange juice, orange rind, baking powder and salt. Gradually mix in flour. Fold in bran flakes and chocolate chips. Drop by teaspoonfuls (5 mL) on ungreased cookie sheets. Bake on middle rack for 10-12 minutes.

Makes about 3 dozen. These cookies freeze well.

L E M O N M U F F I N S

WITH A TANGY LEMON FLAVOR, THIS IS ONE OF MY FAVORITE MUFFINS. BAKE
AND ENJOY!

2 cups	all-purpose flour	500 mL
½ cup	granulated sugar	125 mL
1 tbsp.	baking powder	15 mL
½ tsp.	baking soda	2 mL
1 tsp.	salt	5 mL
1	egg	1
½ cup	melted butter	125 mL
⅓ cup	lemon juice	75 mL
⅔ cup	milk	150 mL
1	lemon, grated rind of	1

Grease muffin tins. Preheat oven to 375°F (190°C). In a large mixing bowl, combine dry ingredients. Make a well in the center of the flour mixture. In a separate bowl, beat egg well. Add butter, lemon juice, milk and lemon rind to egg. Stir well. Pour liquid ingredients into the well of the dry ingredients, stirring until just moistened. Fill greased muffin tins ⅔ full. Bake on middle rack for 18-20 minutes.
Makes 18. These freeze well.

VARIATIONS:

Orange Muffins: Substitute orange juice and orange rind for the lemon.
Add ¾ cup (175 mL) slivered almonds to dry ingredients.

See photograph on page 87.

J A M M U F F I N S

Anyone who likes jam for breakfast will truly enjoy these flavorful muffins. A real treat.

1½ cups	all-purpose flour	375 mL
½ cup	granulated sugar	125 mL
1 tbsp.	baking powder	15 mL
½ tsp.	salt	2 mL
1	egg	1
½ cup	milk	125 mL
¼ cup	melted butter or margarine	60 mL
½ tsp.	vanilla	2 mL
¾ cup	jam or jelly	175 mL

Grease muffin tins. Preheat oven to 375°F (190°C). In a large bowl, combine the flour, sugar, baking powder and salt. Make a well in the center. In a separate bowl, beat egg thoroughly. Stir in milk, melted butter and vanilla. Pour liquid ingredients into the well in the dry ingredients, stirring until just moistened. Fill muffin tins ⅓ full. Spread a teaspoonful (5 mL) of your favorite jam or jelly over batter. Cover with remaining batter, filling tins ⅔ full. Bake on middle rack for 15-17 minutes.
Makes 1 dozen.

CINNAMON SWIRL MUFFINS

THE GREAT TASTE OF CINNAMON MAKES THIS A SUPERB MUFFIN.

½ cup	packed brown sugar	125 mL
2 tsp.	cinnamon	10 mL
1½ cups	all-purpose flour	375 mL
½ cup	granulated sugar	125 mL
1 tbsp.	baking powder	15 mL
½ tsp.	salt	2 mL
1	egg	1
¾ cup	milk	175 mL
¼ cup	melted butter or margarine	60 mL
½ tsp.	vanilla	2 mL

In a small bowl, combine brown sugar and cinnamon. Set aside. Grease muffin tins. Preheat oven to 375°F (190°C). In a large bowl, combine flour, sugar, baking powder and salt. Make a well in the center. In a separate bowl, beat egg thoroughly. Stir in milk, melted butter and vanilla. Pour liquid ingredients into well of dry ingredients, stirring until just moistened. Fill muffin tins ⅓ full. Sprinkle half of cinnamon, sugar mixture over batter. Cover with remaining batter, filling tins ⅔ full. Sprinkle remaining cinnamon mixture over muffins. Bake on middle rack for 15-17 minutes. **Makes 1 dozen.**

See photograph on the back cover.

MAPLE STREUSEL MUFFINS

THIS IS A WONDERFULLY RICH-FLAVORED MUFFIN. THE MAPLE SYRUP SHOULD BE THE REAL THING, NOT AN IMITATION SYRUP. A REAL TREAT.

¼ cup	packed brown sugar	60 mL
1 tsp.	cinnamon	5 mL
2 cups	all-purpose flour	500 mL
¼ cup	wheat germ	60 mL
1 tbsp.	baking powder	15 mL
½ tsp.	salt	2 mL
2	eggs, well beaten	2
½ cup	maple syrup	125 mL
¾ cup	milk	175 mL
¼ cup	melted butter or vegetable oil	60 mL

Grease muffin tins. To make topping, in a small bowl, combine brown sugar and cinnamon. Set aside. Preheat oven to 375°F (190°C). In a large mixing bowl, combine flour, wheat germ, baking powder and salt. Make a well in the center. In a separate bowl, mix eggs, syrup, milk and butter. Pour liquid ingredients into well of dry ingredients, stirring until the dry ingredients are just moistened. Fill muffin tins ⅔ full. Sprinkle the cinnamon/sugar mixture over batter. Bake on middle rack for 20-25 minutes.
Makes 12 large muffins.

VARIATION:

Maple Streusel Nut Muffins: Add ¾ cup (175 mL) of your favorite chopped nuts to the recipe.

CHOCOLATE CHIP MUFFINS

THIS IS A LIGHT, FLUFFY MUFFIN, FULL OF THE RICH, DARK FLAVOR OF CHOCOLATE. IT'S ONE OF MY DAUGHTER'S FAVORITES.

2 cups	all-purpose flour	500 mL
½ cup	granulated sugar	125 mL
3½ tsp.	baking powder	17 mL
½ tsp.	salt	2 mL
1 cup	chocolate chips	250 mL
1	egg	1
1¼ cups	milk	300 mL
¼ cup	melted butter or vegetable oil	60 mL
½ tsp.	vanilla	2 mL

Grease muffin tins. Preheat oven to 375°F (190°C). In a large mixing bowl, combine all dry ingredients. Stir in chocolate chips. Form a well in the center of the flour mixture. In a separate bowl, beat egg well. Add milk, butter and vanilla. Pour liquid mixture into well of dry ingredients, stirring until just moistened. Fill greased muffin tins ⅔ full. Bake on middle rack for 18-20 minutes.
Makes 18 muffins.

VARIATION:

Substitute 1 cup (250 mL) butterscotch or peanut butter chips for the chocolate chips.

C H O C O L A T E M U F F I N S

CHOCOLATE LOVERS WILL ENJOY THESE MUFFINS OFTEN. THEY'RE SO EASY AND A REAL TREAT WHEN YOU'RE IN THE MOOD FOR CHOCOLATE.

2 cups	all-purpose flour	500 mL
½ cup	granulated sugar	125 mL
1 tbsp.	baking powder	15 mL
½ tsp.	salt	2 mL
½ tsp.	baking soda	2 mL
1 cup	milk	250 mL
¼ cup	cocoa	60 mL
2	eggs	2
¼ cup	melted butter or vegetable oil	60 mL
1 tsp.	vanilla	5 mL

Grease muffin tins. Preheat oven to 375°F (190°C). In a large mixing bowl, combine first 5 ingredients. Form a well in the center of the flour mixture. In a separate bowl, combine the milk and cocoa, stirring thoroughly. Add the eggs, melted butter and vanilla to the milk and cocoa. Pour liquid mixture into well of dry ingredients, stirring until just moistened. Fill greased muffin tins ⅔ full. Bake on middle rack for 20-25 minutes.
Makes 12 large muffins. These freeze well.

VARIATIONS:

Double Chocolate Muffins: Add 1 cup (250 mL) of chocolate chips.

Chocolate Nut Muffins: Add 1 cup (250 mL) chopped almonds, pecans or other nuts.

Chocolate Cherry Muffins: Add 1 cup (250 mL) chopped red and/or green maraschino cherries.

B E R R Y   M U F F I N S

THESE MUFFINS CAN BE MADE WITH RASPBERRIES, BLUEBERRIES, HUCKLEBERRIES, OR ANY OF YOUR OTHER FAVORITE BERRIES.

¾ cup	blueberries	175 mL
1 tbsp.	flour	15 mL
2 cups	all-purpose flour	500 mL
1 tbsp.	baking powder	15 mL
½ cup	granulated sugar	125 mL
1 tsp.	salt	5 mL
2	eggs, well beaten	2
1 cup	milk	250 mL
¼ cup	melted butter	60 mL

Grease muffin tins. Preheat oven to 400°F (200°C). Mix berries in 1 tbsp. (15 mL) flour to lightly coat them and set aside. In a large bowl, combine flour, baking powder, sugar and salt. In a separate bowl, combine eggs, milk and butter. Pour into dry ingredients, stirring gently, just until flour is mixed in. Fold in berries. Fill greased muffin tins ⅔ full and bake on middle rack for 15-20 minutes.

Makes 1 dozen large or 18 medium-sized muffins. These freeze well.

See photograph on page 35.

A P P L E S A U C E M U F F I N S

THESE ARE SPICY, DELICIOUS MUFFINS. I MAKE THEM OFTEN FOR MY SON AS HE IS ALLERGIC TO EGGS.

½ cup	butter or margarine	125 mL
1 cup	granulated sugar	250 mL
1½ cups	applesauce	375 mL
2 tsp.	baking soda	10 mL
½ tsp.	salt	2 mL
1 tsp.	cinnamon	5 mL
½ tsp.	nutmeg	2 mL
2 cups	all-purpose flour	500 mL
½ cup	raisins	125 mL

Grease muffin tins. Preheat oven to 375°F (190°C). In a large bowl, cream butter and sugar together. In a small bowl, dissolve baking soda in applesauce. (The applesauce will fizz up a bit.) Stir applesauce into butter mixture. In a separate bowl, combine dry ingredients. Add applesauce mixture to dry ingredients, stirring just until moistened. Fold in raisins. Fill muffin tins ⅔ full and bake on middle rack for 15-20 minutes.
Makes 12 large or 18 smaller muffins. These freeze well.

A P P L E M U F F I N S

APPLES AND CINNAMON ARE AN ALL-TIME FAVORITE FLAVOR COMBINATION.

3 tbsp.	granulated sugar	45 mL
2 tsp.	cinnamon	10 mL
1½ cups	all-purpose flour	375 mL
½ cup	granulated sugar	125 mL
1 tbsp.	baking powder	15 mL
½ tsp.	salt	2 mL
1	egg	1
½ cup	milk	125 mL
¼ cup	melted butter or margarine	60 mL
1 cup	shredded apple, about 2 medium apples	250 mL

Grease muffin tins thoroughly. Preheat oven to 375°F (190°C). In a small bowl, combine 3 tbsp. (45 mL) sugar and the cinnamon. Set aside. In a large bowl, combine flour, sugar, baking powder and salt. Form a well in the center. In a separate bowl, beat egg thoroughly. Stir in milk and melted butter. Fold in apple. Pour liquid mixture into well in dry ingredients, stirring until just moistened. Fill muffin tins ⅔ full. Sprinkle top with sugar, cinnamon mixture. Bake on middle rack for 15-17 minutes.
Makes 1 dozen.

See photograph on page 87.

B A N A N A M U F F I N S

MOIST AND DELICIOUS IS THE ONLY WAY TO DESCRIBE THESE GREAT MUFFINS.

2 cups	all-purpose flour	500 mL
1 cup	granulated sugar	250 mL
2 tsp.	baking powder	10 mL
1 tsp.	baking soda	5 mL
½ tsp.	salt	2 mL
1	egg	1
½ cup	melted butter	125 mL
½ cup	milk	125 mL
1 cup	mashed, ripe banana	250 mL

B A N A N A M U F F I N S

CONTINUED

Grease muffin tins. Preheat oven to 375°F (190°C). In a large mixing bowl, combine dry ingredients. Form a well in the center of the dry ingredients. In a separate bowl, beat egg well. Add butter, milk and banana to egg. Pour liquid ingredients into well in dry ingredients, stirring until just moistened. Fill greased muffin tins ⅔ full. Bake on middle rack for 18-20 minutes. **Makes 18 medium muffins.**

P I N E A P P L E M U F F I N S

THE DELICATE FLAVOR OF PINEAPPLE MAKES THESE MUFFINS A SPECIAL TREAT. THEY ARE ABSOLUTELY DELICIOUS.

2 cups	all-purpose flour	500 mL
½ cup	granulated sugar	125 mL
1 tbsp.	baking powder	15 mL
½ tsp.	salt	2 mL
½ tsp.	baking soda	2 mL
1	egg	1
¼ cup	melted butter	60 mL
1 tsp.	vanilla	5 mL
¾ cup	milk	175 mL
¼ cup	pineapple juice	60 mL
½ cup	drained, crushed pineapple	125 mL

Grease muffin tins. Preheat oven to 375°F (190°C). In a large mixing bowl, combine dry ingredients. Form a well in the center of the flour mixture. In a separate bowl, beat egg thoroughly. Add butter, vanilla, milk, juice and pineapple, stirring well. Pour into well in dry ingredients, stirring until just moistened. Fill greased muffin tins ⅔ full. Bake on middle rack for 18-20 minutes. **Makes 18 muffins.**

P E A C H   M U F F I N S

A DELIGHTFUL MUFFIN WITH SUCH SUPERB FLAVOR THAT IT KEEPS EVERYONE COMING BACK FOR MORE.

¼ cup	packed brown sugar	60 mL
1 tsp.	cinnamon	5 mL
2 cups	all-purpose flour	500 mL
2 tsp.	baking powder	10 mL
1 tsp.	baking soda	5 mL
½ cup	packed brown sugar	125 mL
1 tsp.	salt	5 mL
½ tsp.	cinnamon	2 mL
1	egg	1
½ cup	melted butter	125 mL
¾ cup	milk	175 mL
¼ cup	juice from canned peaches	60 mL
¾ cup	drained, diced canned peaches	175 mL

To make topping, combine ¼ cup (60 mL) brown sugar and 1 tsp. (5 mL) cinnamon. Set aside. Grease muffin tins. Preheat oven to 375°F (190°C). In a large mixing bowl, combine dry ingredients. Form a well in the center of the mixture. In a separate bowl, beat egg well. Add butter, milk, juice and peaches. Stir well. Pour liquid into well of dry ingredients, stirring until just moistened. Fill greased muffin tins ⅔ full. Sprinkle topping on each muffin. Bake on middle rack for 18-20 minutes.
Makes 18 muffins.

RHUBARB CRUMB MUFFINS

WHEN YOU HAVE LOADS OF RHUBARB GROWING IN YOUR GARDEN AND DON'T KNOW WHAT TO DO WITH ALL OF IT, HERE'S A RECIPE THAT WILL HELP USE SOME OF IT UP. IT'S A REALLY GREAT MUFFIN.

¼ cup	packed brown sugar	60 mL
1 tsp.	cinnamon	5 mL
2 cups	all-purpose flour	500 mL
¾ cup	packed brown sugar	175 mL
1 tbsp.	baking powder	15 mL
½ tsp.	baking soda	2 mL
½ tsp.	salt	2 mL
½ tsp.	cinnamon	2 mL
1	egg, well beaten	1
1¼ cups	milk	300 mL
1 tsp.	vanilla	5 mL
¼ cup	melted butter or vegetable oil	60 mL
1 cup	finely chopped rhubarb	250 mL
¾ cup	chopped pecans	175 mL

To make topping, in a small bowl, combine the brown sugar and cinnamon. Set aside. Grease muffin tins. Preheat oven to 375°F (190°C). In a large bowl, combine the flour, sugar, baking powder, soda, salt and cinnamon. Make a well in the center. In a separate bowl, combine egg, milk, vanilla, butter and rhubarb. Pour liquid ingredients into well of dry ingredients, stirring until the dry ingredients are just moistened. Gently stir in the pecans. Fill muffin tins ⅔ full. Bake on middle rack for 20-25 minutes.
Makes 16 medium-sized muffins.

S U N S H I N E   M U F F I N S

THE PINEAPPLE, HONEY AND NUTS MAKE THIS A REALLY DELICIOUS MUFFIN. A REAL CROWD PLEASER.

2 cups	all-purpose flour	500 mL
½ cup	granulated sugar	125 mL
2 tsp.	baking powder	10 mL
1 tsp.	baking soda	5 mL
1 tsp.	cinnamon	5 mL
½ tsp.	nutmeg	2 mL
½ tsp.	salt	2 mL
¼ cup	soft honey	60 mL
2	eggs	2
1 cup	crushed pineapple with juice	250 mL
1 tsp.	vanilla	5 mL
¼ cup	melted butter or vegetable oil	60 mL
¾ cup	grated carrot	175 mL
½ cup	slivered almonds	125 mL
½ cup	sunflower seeds	125 mL

Grease muffin tins. Preheat oven to 375°F (190°C). In a large bowl, combine dry ingredients. Make a well in the center. In a separate bowl, combine the honey, eggs, pineapple, vanilla, butter and carrot. Pour liquid ingredients into well of dry ingredients, stirring until the dry ingredients are just moistened. Add the almonds and sunflower seeds, stirring gently. Fill muffin tins ⅔ full. Bake on middle rack for 20-25 minutes.
Makes 18 muffins.

Breakfast or Brunch, clockwise from lower right

TOP '0 THE MORNING MUFFINS

FULL OF FRUIT AND NUTS, THIS IS A WONDERFUL MUFFIN. GREAT ANYWHERE, ANY TIME.

2 cups	all-purpose flour	500 mL
½ cup	packed brown sugar	125 mL
½ cup	granulated sugar	125 mL
2 tsp.	baking powder	10 mL
1 tsp.	baking soda	5 mL
1 tsp.	cinnamon	5 mL
½ tsp.	salt	2 mL
2	eggs, well beaten	2
1 tsp.	vanilla	5 mL
1¼ cups	milk	300 mL
¼ cup	melted butter or vegetable oil	60 mL
¾ cup	shredded coconut	175 mL
½ cup	chopped pecans	125 mL
½ cup	raisins	125 mL
¾ cup	grated apple	175 mL

Grease muffin tins. Preheat oven to 375°F (190°C). In a large bowl, combine dry ingredients. Make a well in the center. In a separate bowl, combine eggs, vanilla, milk and melted butter. Pour liquid ingredients into well of dry ingredients, stirring until just moistened. Add coconut, pecans, raisins and apple, stirring until just mixed. Fill muffin tins ⅔ full. Bake on middle rack for 20-25 minutes, or until muffins are cooked.
Makes 18 muffins.

P O P P Y   S E E D   M U F F I N S

THE HONEY AND WHEAT GERM ADD A DELICATE TASTE TO THIS RECIPE. A GREAT MUFFIN FOR POPPY SEED LOVERS.

1 cup	milk	250 mL
½ cup	poppy seeds	125 mL
1½ cups	all-purpose flour	375 mL
½ cup	wheat germ	125 mL
1 tbsp.	baking powder	15 mL
2 tbsp.	granulated sugar	30 mL
½ tsp.	salt	2 mL
1	egg	1
¼ cup	melted butter or vegetable oil	60 mL
1 tsp.	vanilla	5 mL
2 tbsp.	soft honey	30 mL

Grease muffin tins. In a small bowl, mix milk and poppy seeds together. Let stand for 10 minutes. Preheat oven to 375°F (190°C). In a large mixing bowl, combine all dry ingredients. Form a well in the center of the flour mixture. Add egg, butter, vanilla and honey to milk/poppy seed mixture. Pour liquid mixture into well of dry ingredients, stirring until just moistened. Fill greased muffin tins ⅔ full. Bake on middle rack for 18-20 minutes. **Makes 12 large muffins. These freeze well.**

See photograph on the back cover.

C O R N M E A L   M U F F I N S

A GREAT MUFFIN WITH A DISTINCTIVE TASTE. THE CORNMEAL GIVES THIS MUFFIN AN ATTRACTIVE YELLOW COLOR. THESE ARE PARTICULARLY GOOD SERVED HOT WITH BUTTER AND MAPLE SYRUP OR HONEY — LIKE TRADITIONAL JOHNNY CAKE.

1¼ cups	all-purpose flour	300 mL
1¼ cups	cornmeal	300 mL
¼ cup	granulated sugar	60 mL
4 tsp.	baking powder	20 mL
½ tsp.	salt	2 mL
1	egg	1
¼ cup	melted butter or vegetable oil	60 mL
1 cup	milk	250 mL
¼ cup	soft honey	60 mL

Grease muffin tins. Preheat oven to 375°F (190°C). In a large mixing bowl, combine dry ingredients. Form a well in the center of the flour mixture. In a separate bowl, beat egg well. Add butter, milk and honey. Stir well. Pour liquid ingredients into well in dry ingredients, stirring until just moistened. Fill greased muffin tins ⅔ full. Bake on middle rack for 18-20 minutes. **Makes 18 muffins. These freeze well.**

T E X - M E X   M U F F I N S

A SAVORY MUFFIN THAT IS A REAL FLAVOR TREAT. THESE MUFFINS ARE A REAL FAVORITE AND MOST PEOPLE CAN'T SEEM TO GET ENOUGH OF THEM.

6	slices bacon, diced	6
½ cup	chopped onion	125 mL
1¼ cups	all-purpose flour	300 mL
1 cup	cornmeal	250 mL
1 tbsp.	granulated sugar	15 mL
1 tbsp.	baking powder	15 mL
1 tsp.	salt	5 mL
1 tsp.	basil	5 mL
½ tsp.	chili powder	2 mL
2	eggs, well beaten	2
1¼ cups	milk	300 mL
¼ cup	melted butter or vegetable oil	60 mL
¾ cup	grated sharp Cheddar cheese	175 mL
¼ cup	diced red pepper	60 mL
¼ cup	diced green pepper	60 mL

Sauté bacon and onion. Drain and set aside. Grease muffin tins. Preheat oven to 375°F (190°C). In a large mixing bowl, combine flour, cornmeal, sugar, baking powder, salt, basil and chili powder. Make a well in the center. In a separate bowl, combine eggs, milk, butter, cheese, peppers, bacon and onion. Pour liquid mixture into well of dry ingredients, stirring until the dry ingredients are just moistened. Fill muffin tins ⅔ full. Bake on middle rack for 20-25 minutes.
Makes 18 medium-sized muffins.

VARIATION:
Add 2-3 tbsp. (30-45 mL) chopped jalapeño peppers.

B R E A K F A S T M U F F I N S

A FABULOUS MUFFIN FOR BREAKFAST OR BRUNCH, WITH FIBER-RICH BRAN. THE BACON, ONIONS AND CHEESE GIVE THIS MUFFIN A SUPERB FLAVOR.

½ lb.	bacon, cut into bite-sized pieces	250 g
½ cup	chopped onion	125 mL
1¾ cups	all-purpose flour	425 mL
¼ cup	granulated sugar	60 mL
1 tbsp.	baking powder	15 mL
½ tsp.	salt	2 mL
½ cup	bran cereal	125 mL
½ cup	shredded Cheddar cheese	125 mL
⅓ cup	vegetable oil or liquid bacon drippings	75 mL
1	egg, well beaten	1
1¼ cups	milk	300 mL

Grease muffin tins. Preheat oven to 375°F (190°C). In a skillet, cook bacon, adding onions during the last 5 minutes. Drain off fat. Set bacon and onions aside. In a large bowl, combine all dry ingredients. Stir well. Add bacon, onions and cheese. Form a well in the center of the flour mixture. In a separate bowl, combine bacon drippings, egg and milk, mixing thoroughly. Pour into well in dry ingredients, stirring until just moistened. Fill muffin tins ⅔ full. Bake on middle rack for 18-20 minutes.
Makes 12 large muffins.

See photograph on page 87.

CHEESY ONION AND DILL MUFFINS

FOR A BREAKFAST THAT IS EASY BUT FLAVORFUL, TRY THESE MUFFINS. THEY
REALLY ARE SUPERB SERVED WARM WITH SAUSAGES.

1	medium onion, diced	1
2 tsp.	butter	10 mL
2 cups	all-purpose flour	500 mL
2 tbsp.	granulated sugar	30 mL
1 tbsp.	baking powder	15 mL
2 tsp.	dillweed	10 mL
1 tsp.	onion salt	5 mL
½ tsp.	celery salt	2 mL
½ tsp.	salt	2 mL
2	eggs, well beaten	2
1 cup	sour cream	250 mL
¾ cup	milk	175 mL
¼ cup	melted butter or vegetable oil	60 mL
¾ cup	grated, sharp Cheddar cheese	175 mL

In a skillet, sauté the onion in 2 tsp. (10 mL) of butter. Drain and set aside.
Grease muffin tins. Preheat oven to 375°F (190°C). In a large bowl, combine
the dry ingredients. Make a well in the center. In a separate bowl, combine
the liquid ingredients and the onion. Pour liquid ingredients into well of dry
ingredients, stirring until the dry ingredients are just moistened. Fill muffin
tins ⅔ full. Bake on middle rack for 20-25 minutes.
Makes 18 medium-sized muffins.

C H E E S Y   A P P L E   M U F F I N S

CHEESE AND APPLE HAVE ALWAYS BEEN A GREAT COMBINATION. WITH THE
ADDITION OF RAISINS, THESE MUFFINS BECOME A REALLY SPECIAL TREAT.

1 cup	all-purpose flour	250 mL
1 cup	whole-wheat flour	250 mL
½ cup	rolled oats	125 mL
½ cup	packed brown sugar	125 mL
1 tbsp.	baking powder	15 mL
1 tsp.	salt	5 mL
1 tsp.	cinnamon	5 mL
½ tsp.	nutmeg	2 mL
2	eggs, well beaten	2
1¼ cups	milk	300 mL
1 tsp.	vanilla	5 mL
⅓ cup	melted butter or vegetable oil	75 mL
1 cup	grated apple	250 mL
¾ cup	raisins	175 mL
½ cup	grated, sharp Cheddar cheese	125 mL

Grease muffin tins. Preheat oven to 375°F (190°C). In a large bowl, combine
the dry ingredients. Make a well in the center. In a separate bowl, combine
eggs, milk, vanilla, butter, apple, raisins and cheese. Pour liquid ingredients
into well of dry ingredients, stirring until the dry ingredients are just
moistened. Fill muffin tins ⅔ full. Bake on middle rack for 20-25 minutes.
Makes 24 muffins.

RAISIN OATMEAL MUFFINS

WITH RAISINS AND ROLLED OATS, THERE'S LOTS OF GOODNESS IN THESE.

1 cup	all-purpose flour	250 mL
3½ tsp.	baking powder	17 mL
½ cup	packed brown sugar	125 mL
½ tsp.	salt	2 mL
½ tsp.	cinnamon	2 mL
¼ tsp.	nutmeg	1 mL
¾ cup	rolled oats	175 mL
¾ cup	raisins	175 mL
1	egg	1
1 cup	milk	250 mL
¼ cup	melted butter or vegetable oil	60 mL

Grease muffin tins. Preheat oven to 375°F (190°C). In a large mixing bowl, combine dry ingredients. Add raisins and stir well. Make a well in the center of the flour mixture. In a separate bowl, beat egg well. Add milk and butter. Pour liquid into well in dry ingredients, stirring until just moistened. Fill greased muffin tins ⅔ full. Bake on middle rack for 18-20 minutes.
Makes 12 large muffins. These freeze well.

CRANBERRY OAT MUFFINS

A GREAT MUFFIN TREAT WITH THE TANGY TASTE OF CRANBERRIES. THE
ROLLED OATS PROVIDE ADDED GOODNESS.

1½ cups	all-purpose flour	375 mL
1 cup	rolled oats	250 mL
½ cup	packed brown sugar	125 mL
1 tbsp.	baking powder	15 mL
1 tsp.	salt	5 mL
1 tsp.	cinnamon	5 mL
1 cup	chopped cranberries or whole wild cranberries	250 mL
1	egg	1
¼ cup	melted butter or vegetable oil	60 mL
1 cup	milk	250 mL

Grease muffin tins. Preheat oven to 375°F (190°C). In a large mixing bowl,
combine all dry ingredients and cranberries. Make a well in center. In a
separate bowl, beat egg well. Add milk and melted butter to egg. Mix well.
Pour liquid mixture into well in dry ingredients, stirring until just moistened.
Drop into muffin tins, filling tins ⅔ full. Bake on middle rack for 18-20
minutes.
Makes 12 large muffins. These freeze well.

VARIATION:

Add ¾ cup (175 mL) of chopped nuts of your choice to dry ingredients.

See photograph on page 87.

STRAWBERRY DELIGHT MUFFINS

FRESH STRAWBERRIES MAKE THIS A WONDERFUL MUFFIN THAT EVERYONE WILL ENJOY. ONCE YOU'VE MADE THESE, YOU'LL WANT THEM AGAIN AND AGAIN.

1½ cups	all-purpose flour	375 mL
¾ cup	rolled oats	175 mL
¼ cup	wheat germ	60 mL
¼ cup	granulated sugar	60 mL
¼ cup	packed brown sugar	60 mL
2 tsp.	baking powder	10 mL
1 tsp.	baking soda	5 mL
½ tsp.	salt	2 mL
½ tsp.	nutmeg	2 mL
1	egg, well beaten	1
1¼ cups	milk	300 mL
1 tsp.	vanilla	5 mL
¼ cup	melted butter or vegetable oil	60 mL
1 cup	chopped, fresh strawberries	250 mL

Grease muffin tins. Preheat oven to 375°F (190°C). In a large mixing bowl, combine dry ingredients. Make a well in the center. In a separate bowl, combine liquid ingredients and strawberries. Pour liquid mixture into well of dry ingredients, stirring until the dry ingredients are just moistened. Fill muffin tins ⅔ full. Bake on middle rack for 20-25 minutes.
Makes 12 large muffins.

VARIATION:

Strawberry Nut Muffins: Add ¾ cup (175 mL) of your favorite chopped nuts to the recipe.

STRAWBERRY BANANA MUFFINS

STRAWBERRIES AND BANANAS REALLY DO MAKE A WONDERFUL COMBINATION. THIS IS SUCH A GREAT MUFFIN, IT'S A WINNER EVERY TIME.

1 cup	all-purpose flour	250 mL
1 cup	whole-wheat flour	250 mL
¾ cup	granulated sugar	175 mL
1 tbsp.	baking powder	15 mL
½ tsp.	baking soda	2 mL
½ tsp.	salt	2 mL
½ tsp.	allspice	2 mL
¾ cup	chopped almonds	175 mL
2	eggs, well beaten	2
¾ cup	mashed fresh strawberries	175 mL
½ cup	mashed banana	125 mL
¼ cup	milk	60 mL
1 tsp.	vanilla	5 mL
¼ cup	melted butter or vegetable oil	60 mL

Grease muffin tins. Preheat oven to 375°F (190°C). In a large mixing bowl, combine dry ingredients and almonds. Make a well in the center. In a separate bowl, combine eggs, strawberries, banana, milk, vanilla and butter. Pour liquid mixture into well of dry ingredients, stirring just until the dry ingredients are moistened. Fill muffin tins ⅔ full. Bake on middle rack for 20-25 minutes.
Makes 18 muffins.

B A N A N A   O A T   M U F F I N S

THIS IS A MOIST, RICH MUFFIN. A REAL DELIGHT.

2 cups	all-purpose flour	500 mL
1 cup	rolled oats	250 mL
½ cup	granulated sugar	125 mL
2 tsp.	baking powder	10 mL
1 tsp.	baking soda	5 mL
½ tsp.	salt	2 mL
2	eggs	2
¼ cup	melted butter or vegetable oil	60 mL
¾ cup	milk	175 mL
1 cup	mashed ripe banana	250 mL

Grease muffin tins. Preheat oven to 375°F (190°C). In a large mixing bowl, combine dry ingredients. Form a well in the center of the dry ingredients. In a separate bowl, beat eggs well. Stir in butter, milk and banana. Pour liquid ingredients into well in dry ingredients, stirring until just moistened. Fill greased muffin tins ⅔ full. Bake on middle rack for 18-20 minutes.
Makes 18 medium muffins.

A P R I C O T   M U F F I N S

DRIED APRICOTS AND SPICES GIVE THIS MUFFIN A DISTINCTIVE TASTE.

1 cup	all-purpose flour	250 mL
1 tbsp.	baking powder	15 mL
½ cup	packed brown sugar	125 mL
½ tsp.	salt	2 mL
½ tsp.	cinnamon	2 mL
¼ tsp.	nutmeg	1 mL
¾ cup	rolled oats	175 mL
¾ cup	chopped, dried apricots	175 mL
1	egg	1
1 cup	milk	250 mL
¼ cup	melted butter or vegetable oil	60 mL

A P R I C O T   M U F F I N S

CONTINUED

Grease muffin tins. Preheat oven to 375°F (190°C). In a large bowl, combine dry ingredients. Stir in apricots. Form a well in the center of the flour mixture. In a separate bowl, beat egg well. Add milk and butter. Pour into well in dry ingredients, stirring until just moistened. Fill greased muffin tins ⅔ full. Bake on middle rack for 18-20 minutes.
Makes 12 large muffins.

See photograph on page 87.

O A T M E A L   N U T   M U F F I N S

A WHOLESOME MUFFIN, GREAT FOR BREAKFASTS OR SNACKS.

1 cup	all-purpose flour	250 mL
3½ tsp.	baking powder	17 mL
½ cup	packed brown sugar	125 mL
½ tsp.	salt	2 mL
½ tsp.	cinnamon	2 mL
¼ tsp.	nutmeg	1 mL
¾ cup	rolled oats	175 mL
¾ cup	chopped nuts of your choice	175 mL
1	egg	1
1 cup	milk	250 mL
¼ cup	melted butter or vegetable oil	60 mL

Grease muffin tins. Preheat oven to 375°F (190°C). In a large mixing bowl, combine dry ingredients. Stir in nuts. Form a well in the center of the flour mixture. In a separate bowl, beat egg well. Stir in milk and butter. Pour liquid ingredients into well in dry ingredients, stirring until just moistened. Fill greased muffin tins ⅔ full. Bake on middle rack for 18-20 minutes.
Makes 12 muffins. These freeze well.

G I N G E R B R E A D   M U F F I N S

A DARK AND DELICIOUS MUFFIN WITH THE FLAVOR OF GINGERBREAD AND THE
ADDED GOODNESS OF FIBER-RICH ROLLED OATS.

2 cups	all-purpose flour	500 mL
2 tsp.	baking powder	10 mL
¼ cup	granulated sugar	60 mL
1 tsp.	baking soda	5 mL
½ tsp.	salt	2 mL
2 tsp.	ginger	10 mL
1 cup	rolled oats	250 mL
1	egg	1
¼ cup	melted butter	60 mL
½ cup	molasses	125 mL
1 cup	hot water	250 mL

Grease muffin tins. Preheat oven to 375°F (190°C). In a large bowl, combine
dry ingredients and mix well. Form a well in the center of the flour mixture.
In a separate bowl, beat egg well. Add butter, molasses and water. Pour liquid
mixture into well of dry ingredients, stirring until just moistened. Fill greased
muffin tins ⅔ full. Bake on middle rack for 18-20 minutes.
Makes 18 muffins.

S P I C Y   P U M P K I N   M U F F I N S

A DELICIOUS MUFFIN WITH CINNAMON AND NUTMEG ENHANCING THE
PUMPKIN FLAVOR. PREPARE AND ENJOY!

1¼ cups	all-purpose flour	300 mL
¼ cup	granulated sugar	60 mL
1 tbsp.	baking powder	15 mL
½ tsp.	salt	2 mL
1 tsp.	cinnamon	5 mL
½ tsp.	nutmeg	2 mL
1 cup	rolled oats	250 mL
1	egg	1
⅔ cup	canned or fresh, cooked, mashed pumpkin	150 mL
⅓ cup	milk	75 mL
¼ cup	melted butter or vegetable oil	60 mL

Grease muffin tins. Preheat oven to 375°F (190°C). In a large mixing bowl,
combine dry ingredients. Form a well in center. In a separate bowl, beat egg
well. Stir in pumpkin, milk and butter. Pour into the well in dry ingredients,
stirring until just moistened. Fill muffin tins ⅔ full. Bake on middle rack for
18-20 minutes.
Makes 12 large muffins.

VARIATION:

Add ¾ cup (175 mL) of nuts of your choice to dry ingredients.

SPICY ZUCCHINI MUFFINS

A GREAT WAY TO USE UP SOME OF THE ZUCCHINI FROM YOUR GARDEN. THESE MUFFINS FILL THE HOUSE WITH THE WONDERFUL AROMA OF SPICES AND THEY TASTE GREAT TOO.

1½ cups	all-purpose flour	375 mL
½ cup	rolled oats	125 mL
¼ cup	wheat germ	60 mL
½ cup	packed brown sugar	125 mL
2 tsp.	baking powder	10 mL
1 tsp.	baking soda	5 mL
½ tsp.	salt	2 mL
1 tsp.	cinnamon	5 mL
½ tsp.	nutmeg	2 mL
½ tsp.	cloves	2 mL
½ tsp.	allspice	2 mL
1	egg, well beaten	1
1 tsp.	vanilla	5 mL
1¼ cups	milk	300 mL
¼ cup	melted butter or vegetable oil	60 mL
1 cup	grated zucchini	250 mL

Grease muffin tins. Preheat oven to 375°F (190°C). In a large mixing bowl, combine dry ingredients. Make a well in center. In a separate bowl, combine the egg, vanilla, milk, butter and zucchini. Pour liquid ingredients into well of dry ingredients, stirring until the dry ingredients are just moistened. Fill muffin tins ⅔ full. Bake on middle rack for 20-25 minutes.
Makes 18 muffins.

VARIATION:

Zucchini Bran Muffins: Substitute ½ cup (125 mL) of bran flakes for the rolled oats.
Zucchini Nut Muffins: Add ¾ cup (175 mL) of your favorite chopped nuts to the recipe.

SPICY CARROT MUFFINS

THE RICH AROMA OF CINNAMON FILLS THE KITCHEN WHEN THESE MUFFINS ARE BAKING. THEY ARE MOIST, SPICY AND FULL OF WHOLESOME GOODNESS WITH BRAN, WHEAT GERM AND CARROT.

1½ cups	all-purpose flour	375 mL
½ cup	bran flakes	125 mL
¼ cup	wheat germ	60 mL
½ cup	packed brown sugar	125 mL
2 tsp.	baking soda	10 mL
1 tsp.	baking powder	5 mL
½ tsp.	salt	2 mL
1 tsp.	cinnamon	5 mL
½ tsp.	nutmeg	2 mL
1	egg	1
2 tbsp.	molasses	30 mL
¼ cup	melted butter or vegetable oil	60 mL
1¼ cups	milk	300 mL
1 cup	grated carrot	250 mL

Grease muffin tins. Preheat oven to 375°F (190°C). In a large mixing bowl, combine all dry ingredients. Form a well in the center of the dry ingredients. In a separate bowl, beat egg thoroughly. Stir molasses, butter, milk and grated carrot into egg. Pour liquid ingredients into well in dry ingredients, stirring until just moistened. Fill greased muffin tins ⅔ full. Bake on middle rack for 18-20 minutes.
Makes 12-14 muffins.

See photograph on page 69.

H O T   C R O S S   M U F F I N S

THIS IS TRULY A DELICIOUS MUFFIN. EASY TO MAKE AND GREAT TO TASTE, IT'S A REAL FAVORITE AT OUR HOUSE.

14 oz.	can pineapple bits with juice	398 mL
	milk	
1 cup	bran flakes	250 mL
1	egg, well beaten	1
⅓ cup	melted butter or vegetable oil	75 mL
1 tsp.	vanilla	5 mL
½ cup	quartered red and green cherries	125 mL
1½ cups	all-purpose flour	375 mL
½ cup	packed brown sugar	125 mL
1 tbsp.	baking powder	15 mL
2 tsp.	cinnamon	10 mL
½ tsp.	salt	2 mL
½ tsp.	allspice	2 mL
¼ tsp.	cloves	1 mL
½ cup	fruit peel	125 mL
½ cup	raisins	125 mL
½ cup	chopped pecans or almonds	125 mL

GLAZE

½ cup	icing sugar	125 mL
3-4 tsp.	milk	15-20 mL

Grease muffin tins. Preheat oven to 375°F (190°C). Drain pineapple juice into measuring cup. Add milk to make 1 cup (250 mL). (Milk will sour.) Set aside the pineapple. Combine the juice/milk, and the bran flakes. Let stand for about 10 minutes. Stir in the egg, butter and vanilla. Add the pineapple and cherries. In a separate bowl, combine the dry ingredients, fruit peel, raisins and nuts. Make a well in the center. Pour liquid ingredients into well of dry ingredients, stirring until the dry ingredients are just moistened. Fill muffin tins ⅔ full. Bake on middle rack for 20-25 minutes. When muffins are cool, combine icing sugar and milk. Drizzle the glaze over the muffins. **Makes about 16 medium-sized muffins.**

HONEY OAT AND BRAN MUFFINS

ONE OF THE MOST FIBER-RICH MUFFINS OF ALL TIME. A VERY HEALTHY MUFFIN WITH GREAT TASTE.

½ cup	bran cereal	125 mL
1 cup	rolled oats	250 mL
¾ cup	wheat germ	175 mL
1 tsp.	cinnamon	5 mL
½ tsp.	salt	2 mL
1 cup	buttermilk or sour milk, see page 20	250 mL
2	eggs	2
¾ cup	soft honey	175 mL
½ cup	melted butter	125 mL
1 cup	all-purpose flour	250 mL
2 tsp.	baking powder	10 mL
1 tsp.	baking soda	5 mL

Grease muffin tins. Preheat oven to 375°F (190°C). In a large bowl, mix bran, rolled oats, wheat germ, cinnamon, salt and milk. Let stand for ½ hour. Beat egg and add to milk mixture. Add honey and butter. In a separate bowl, combine flour, baking powder and baking soda. Add to liquid ingredients, stirring until just moistened. Fill greased muffin tins ⅔ full. Bake on middle rack for 18-20 minutes.

Makes 18 muffins. These freeze well.

H O N E Y B R A N M U F F I N S

FIBER-RICH MUFFINS WITH A DELICIOUS FLAVOR. A REAL TREAT.

1¼ cups	milk	300 mL
1½ cups	bran cereal	375 mL
1	egg	1
⅓ cup	melted butter or vegetable oil	75 mL
½ cup	soft honey	125 mL
1¼ cups	all-purpose flour	300 mL
1 tbsp.	baking powder	15 mL
½ tsp.	salt	2 mL

Grease muffin tins. Preheat oven to 375°F (190°C). Stir bran into milk and let stand for 10 minutes. Add egg, butter and honey to milk/bran mixture. In a separate bowl, combine dry ingredients and form well in center. Pour liquid mixture into well, stirring until just moistened. Fill greased muffin tins ⅔ full. Bake on middle rack for 18-20 minutes.
Makes 12 large muffins. These freeze well.

VARIATIONS:

Add ¾ cup (175 mL) chopped, dried apples and 1 tsp. (5 mL) of cinnamon to the recipe.

Add ¾ cup (175 mL) chopped nuts of your choice.

B R A N   M U F F I N S

AN ALL-TIME FAVORITE MUFFIN THAT IS RICH IN FIBER AND TRULY DELICIOUS TO EAT.

1 cup	buttermilk or sour milk	250 mL
1 cup	bran	250 mL
1 cup	flour	250 mL
¼ cup	packed brown sugar	60 mL
2 tsp.	baking powder	10 mL
1 tsp.	baking soda	5 mL
½ tsp.	salt	2 mL
¾ cup	raisins	175 mL
½ cup	melted butter or margarine	125 mL
1	egg, beaten	1
3 tbsp.	molasses	45 mL

Grease muffin tins. Preheat oven to 375°F (190°C). Combine milk and bran. Allow to stand for 10 minutes. In a large mixing bowl, combine all dry ingredients. Stir in raisins. Form a well in the center of the dry ingredients. Add butter, egg and molasses to milk and bran mixture. Pour liquid mixture into well in dry ingredients, stirring until just moistened. Fill greased muffin tins ⅔ full. Bake on middle rack for 18-20 minutes.
Makes 12 large muffins. These freeze well.

BANANA BRAN MUFFINS

HIGH IN FIBER AND RICH IN FLAVOR, THIS MUFFIN IS A REAL WINNER.

1 cup	all-purpose flour	250 mL
1 cup	All-Bran	250 mL
½ cup	granulated sugar	125 mL
2 tsp.	baking powder	10 mL
1 tsp.	baking soda	5 mL
½ tsp.	salt	2 mL
2	eggs	2
¼ cup	melted butter or vegetable oil	60 mL
½ cup	sour milk, see page 20	125 mL
1 cup	mashed ripe banana	250 mL

Grease muffin tins. Preheat oven to 375°F (190°C). In a large mixing bowl, combine dry ingredients. Form a well in the center of the dry ingredients. In a separate bowl, beat eggs well. Stir in butter, milk and banana. Pour liquid mixture into well in dry ingredients, stirring until just moistened. Fill greased muffin tins ⅔ full. Bake on middle rack for 18-20 minutes.
Makes 12 large muffins.

CITRUS AND RAISIN BRAN MUFFINS

WHOLESOME AND DELICIOUS. THIS MUFFIN IS FULL OF FIBER AND TASTES GREAT TOO.

¾ cup	bran flakes	175 mL
¾ cup	rolled oats	175 mL
¾ cup	wheat germ	175 mL
1 tsp.	cinnamon	5 mL
1 cup	sour milk, see page 20	250 mL
2	eggs, well beaten	2
¾ cup	soft honey	175 mL
¼ cup	orange juice	60 mL
1 tbsp.	lemon juice	15 mL
1 tsp.	vanilla	5 mL
½ cup	melted butter or vegetable oil	125 mL
1 cup	all-purpose flour	250 mL
2 tsp.	baking powder	10 mL
1 tsp.	baking soda	5 mL
½ tsp.	salt	2 mL
¾ cup	raisins	175 mL

In a large bowl, combine bran, oats, wheat germ, cinnamon and sour milk. Let stand for about 15 minutes. Grease muffin tins. Preheat oven to 375°F (190°C). Beat egg and add to bran mixture. Add honey, juices, vanilla and butter. In a large, separate bowl, combine flour, baking powder, baking soda, salt and raisins. Make a well in the center. Pour liquid ingredients into well of dry ingredients, stirring until dry ingredients are just moistened. Fill muffin tins ⅔ full. Bake on middle rack for 20-25 minutes.
Makes 18 medium-sized muffins. These freeze well.

VARIATION:

Citrus Nut Muffins: Replace ¾ cup (175 mL) of raisins with ¾ cup (175 mL) of your favorite chopped nuts.

O R A N G E B R A N M U F F I N S

A MUFFIN FULL OF FIBER-RICH GOODNESS. WHOLESOME AND DELICIOUS.

1 cup	all-purpose flour	250 mL
1 cup	All-Bran	250 mL
½ cup	packed brown sugar	125 mL
2 tsp.	baking powder	10 mL
1 tsp.	baking soda	5 mL
½ tsp.	salt	2 mL
¼ tsp.	nutmeg	1 mL
1	egg	1
¼ cup	melted butter or vegetable oil	60 mL
¾ cup	buttermilk or sour milk, see page 20	175 mL
5 tbsp.	orange juice	75 mL
1	orange, grated rind of	1

Grease muffin tins. Preheat oven to 375°F (190°C). In a large mixing bowl, combine dry ingredients. Form a well in the center of the dry ingredients. In a separate bowl, beat egg well. Stir in butter, buttermilk, orange juice and orange rind. Pour liquid ingredients into well in dry ingredients, stirring until dry ingredients are just moistened. Fill greased muffin tins ⅔ full. Bake on middle rack for 18-20 minutes.
Makes 12 large muffins. These freeze well.

See photograph on page 87.

I N D E X

Muffins

A FAMILY TRADITION

Marg Ruttan, her brother Lew Miller and her daughter Stacy have been cooking for as long as they can remember. That's not surprising, however, since cooking professionally has been a part of their family history for almost 150 years.

Marg's and Lew's paternal great-grandfather, James Miller, who was born in 1846, was a professional cook. He earned his living cooking in lumber camps and any venue that needed his services. In the tradition of the time, his twelve sons went to work with him as helpers and, in the process, learned his trade. Not all of them earned their living as cooks, but some did and all could. To this day, progeny of that line are professional chefs.

Marg's and Lew's paternal grandmother, Charlotte Harbour, worked as a housekeeper/cook prior to her marriage. She was an excellent baker and, as she lived with Marg and Lew, both have been influenced by her teaching, especially Lew. It is significant too, that in his retirement years, their father has become involved in the world of food and its preparation.

On their mother's side of the family there were also professional cooks. Their grandfather's only brother was a cook and his two sons earned their living in the food industry; one as a cook and the other as a restaurant owner and cook. Some of their children have also become professional chefs.

But it is their maternal grandmother to whom Marg and Lew ascribe much of their love affair with food. In 1902, Margaret Robin, then a young woman of 17, sailed from her home at Gaspe, Quebec, to Schenectady, New York, to stay with her brother Frank and his wife Nora, to assist them after the birth of their first child. Later, Margaret, affectionately known as Maggie, decided to stay in Schenectady and went to work for a doctor and his family as a cook/housekeeper. The good doctor and his wife, seeing potential in Maggie's ability with food, arranged for her to attend a cooking school for two years while she continued to work part time for them. When she completed her schooling, Maggie stayed on with her mentors for some time.

Eventually she returned to Gaspe, where she continued her career as a cook, working in hotels, restaurants and lumber camps. More importantly, though, she possessed creativity and an instinct for how best to prepare and serve any food to enhance its unique flavors and textures.

Lew remembers a day when he and grandfather brought home a baby halibut, fresh from the waters of the bay. Grandma took one look and promptly issued orders for the fish to be cleaned and brought to her. Meanwhile, she prepared a sage and onion dressing for the fish and it was stuffed and baked, then served up with boiled new potatoes and garden-fresh peas; a deceptively simple yet perfect meal.

She did many things. Among them she baked wedding cakes, dark, heavy and laden with fruit. She decorated them too. Such a fruit cake might become the prize of a raffle or other game of chance, or be auctioned off to make money for some worthy cause. That tradition persists. Both daughters have baked fruit cakes, often used for weddings, as have Lew and Marg.

The tradition of cooking continued with some of Maggie's children. Her sons Tommy and Russell were both professional cooks and Marg's and Lew's mum, Esther, also became a cook. Current generations include good home cooks, passionate about food and cooking, as well as professional cooks and chefs. During a recent conversation with a cousin, who told about her son's love of baking cookies, Lew commented that the young lad must be vaccinated with the Maggie needle. Well perhaps that's it, they're all inoculated with it. Certainly the tradition continues.

With such a strong heritage in the food industry, it seems only fitting that Marg, Lew and Stacy should continue to develop and pass on the family tradition. They truly love to prepare the old favorite family recipes and do so frequently. They've discovered, however, that their passion for creating and developing new and interesting recipes, which then become a part of the family tradition, is the real impetus in their love affair with food.

How fitting that their series of cookbooks should be called *Traditions of Home*, for that is exactly what the recipes are – family traditions, both new and old. Born of generations of cooks, Marg, Lew and Stacy present recipes that are a pleasure to make and a delight to serve. Recipes full of homemade goodness and flavor – yours to enjoy. You'll want to make them part of your family tradition.

A Gift of Tradition

Cookies & Muffins _____ x $10.95 = $ _____

Casseroles, Soups & More _____ x $10.95 = $ _____

Around My Kitchen Table _____ x $7.95 = $ _____

Postage and handling (total order)_____ = $ _____ 3.00

Subtotal _____ = $ _____

In Canada add 7% GST _____(Subtotal x .07) = $ _____

Total enclosed_____ = $ _____

U.S. and international orders payable in U.S. funds./ Price is subject to change.

NAME: _____

STREET: _____

CITY: _____ PROV./STATE _____

COUNTRY _____ POSTAL CODE/ZIP _____

Please make cheque or money order payable to: **Traditions of Home Publishing**
5134 – 13th Avenue
Edson, Alberta
Canada   T7E 1H5

For fund raising or volume purchases, contact **Traditions of Home Publishing** for volume rates.
Please allow 2-3 weeks for delivery

A Gift of Tradition

Cookies & Muffins _____ x $10.95 = $ _____

Casseroles, Soups & More _____ x $10.95 = $ _____

Around My Kitchen Table _____ x $7.95 = $ _____

Postage and handling (total order)_____ = $ _____ 3.00

Subtotal _____ = $ _____

In Canada add 7% GST _____(Subtotal x .07) = $ _____

Total enclosed_____ = $ _____

U.S. and international orders payable in U.S. funds./ Price is subject to change.

NAME: _____

STREET: _____

CITY: _____ PROV./STATE _____

COUNTRY _____ POSTAL CODE/ZIP _____

Please make cheque or money order payable to: **Traditions of Home Publishing**
5134 – 13th Avenue
Edson, Alberta
Canada   T7E 1H5

For fund raising or volume purchases, contact **Traditions of Home Publishing** for volume rates.
Please allow 2-3 weeks for delivery

Around My Kitchen Table

by Marg Ruttan

This collection of bits of wit and wisdom was gathered over a lifetime of experience and observation in discussions around a family's kitchen table. Chosen to enrich our lives, some bits bring smiles; some are profound and become vehicles of change; some produce both smiles and change. These insights are sure to delight, amuse and touch a responsive chord.

Retail $7.95   4½" x 6"
144 pages   20 line drawings
                                                  perfect bound

Traditions of Home – Casseroles, Soups & More

by Marg Ruttan, Stacy Ruttan and Lew Miller

Another heart-warming addition to the *Traditions of Home* series of books, *Casseroles, Soups & More* contains a bounty of hearty and comforting recipes. There are old-fashioned family favorites and new recipes destined to become family favorites. Many of these casseroles and soups are one-dish main-course meals, convenient to make and serve. With the addition of a salad and bread or buns, you can create a lunch or dinner for the most elegant or casual occasion. Every day is the perfect time to enjoy the satisfying flavors and aromas of *Casseroles, Soups & More.*

Retail $10.95   6" x 9"
120 pages   6 coloured photographs

Watch for *Traditions of Home – Breads & More*
projected publication date January 1996.